Roses
A Popular Guide

Mark Mattock

BLANDFORD PRESS
Poole   Dorset

First published in the U.K. 1980

Copyright © 1980 Blandford Press Ltd
Link House, West Street, Poole, Dorset, BH15 1LL

British Library Cataloguing in Publication Data

Mattock, Mark
  Roses.
  1. Roses
  I. Title
  635.9′33′372   SB411

ISBN 0 7137 0914 6

Filmset by Keyspools Ltd, Golborne, Lancashire.
Printed in Hong Kong
by South China Printing Co.

Contents

Acknowledgements

To acknowledge fully the help given by friends and acquaintances from all corners of the world in preparing this book, and to mention by name all those whose words of wisdom I have listened to, or read, would fill more lines than my publishers will allow; and even then I might inadvertently omit someone. May I, however, select from the World of Roses the following:

Sam McGredy (New Zealand), Reimer Kordes (Germany), Niels Poulsen and his family (Denmark), Len Turner and Josie Shepherd (Royal National Rose Society), The Council and Members of the Royal National Rose Society, Dr Alfred S. Thomas (Australia), Dr B. P. Pal, F.R.S. (India), J. B. Wise (South Africa), Dr A. C. T. Campbell (Australia), Leslie Mitchell (Republic of Ireland), Wini and Fred Edmunds (USA).

Thanks are of course due to the members of the Mattock family and the staff of John Mattock Ltd and particularly to my wife Jean, who not only saw this book through from its inception to its completion, but also who, with infinite patience, typed it in its many draft forms.

To the above mentioned, and to those others whose help throughout in a life of Roses, I am most grateful.

Photographic Acknowledgements

A–Z Photographic Collection 65, 143, 169; R. H. Barrett 17, 18; Dr A. C. T. Campbell (Australia) 32; Cants of Colchester 53; Wini and Fred Edmunds (USA) 28, 29; Harkness Roses, Hitchin, Herts. 39, 47; Jarrolds 63, 114; Kordes Sohne, Sparrieshoop, West Germany 23, 37, 44, 57, 87, 89, 95, 100, 101, 117, 131, 137, 159; James M. Mattock 147; John S. Mattock 155, 171, 173; John Mattock Ltd 25, 27, 35, 55, 61, 75, 88, 165; M. W. Mattock 157, 161; The Sam McGredy collection 49, 59, 67, 73, 81, 83, 91, 93, 103, 115, 121, 127, 129, 133, 135; Dr B. P. Pal, FRS 31; Poulsen 71; Harry Smith 41, 51, 97, 111, 119, 123, 125, 139, 141, 145, 149, 151, 153, 163, 164, 167; Dr Alfred S. Thomas OBE 33; Bryan Tysterman 43, 69, 79, 85, 99, 105, 107, 109, 113; Universal Rose Selection (Meilland) France 21, 77, 116; J. B. Wise, South Africa 30; Craig Wallace, Belfast, Northern Ireland 19.

Introduction

The Rose

The evolution of the Rose having taken place with the help of man has been recorded, from the dawn of written history to modern times, either in the written word or portrayed by the artist.

One of the most exciting adventure tales of intrigue and travel concerns the Rose in all its forms. The mercenaries of the armies of Sargon, ruler of Sumeria and Akkad some five thousand years ago, long before the formation of the great Persian Empires, brought back specimens of the Rose from their forays over the Taurus, for the delectation of their masters, to decorate palace gardens and walks in the delta of the Euphrates and Tigris.

Theophratus of ancient Greece, the 'father' of botany, mentions Roses having from five to one hundred petals, the species roses or briars still to be found in many a garden, and what is thought to be *R. centifolia*.

The early Romans, Seneca and Pliny, both wrote of growing Roses in specially constructed hot houses to force blooms during the winter. Pliny's *Natural History* contains references to twelve Roses, among which are thought to be forms of *R. alba, R. canina, R. centifolia, R. damascena* and *R. gallica*.

The inclusion of plants in the booty of the early conquerors and subsequent distribution, accounts for the appearances at different times and in divers places of the early forms of the Rose. Indeed, although some varieties were 'lost' in the years immediately after the fall of the Roman Empire, the spread of Islam in the Mediterranean areas, reintroduced them from Persia and the Middle East.

In Europe the medicinal use of the flower ensured a record of its survival. In AD 550, King Childebert in Paris, had a Rose garden constructed for his wife with the same varieties which the Romans had brought. It is said that Charlemagne planted Roses in his garden. But we have to wait until very much later before the Rose became, once more, 'The Queen of Flowers'.

It is difficult to place in order, either of time or importance, the sequence of events which brought this about. Commerce and religion both had a great influence. Merchants and their agents vied with each other in sending back from their travels exotic specimens to their patrons. Among their introductions we can number the famous Banksian Roses, and even more important the influential (upon later Rose breeding) China Roses.

The collection into one garden, at her palace of Malmaison, by the Empress Josephine, of all the Roses existing in her day, is famous not only for the emergence of the great names of Redouté, her court flower painter, and Dupont, who collected and planted the garden, but also, strangest of all, for the appearance of Kennedy, an English nurseryman who, despite the enmity between France and England, was allowed to come and go between the two countries with Rose plants.

In the United States of America, John Champney of Charleston created the *Noisette* class, important in its day for its influence on the production of remontant, or repeat flowering varieties.

Bibliography

Bunyard, Edward A. (1936) *Old Garden Roses*, Country Life, London

Edwards, Gordon (1962/73) *Roses for Enjoyment*, David & Charles, Newton Abbot

Edwards, Gordon (1974) *Wild and Old Garden Roses*, David & Charles, Newton Abbot

Fairbrother, F. (1962) *Roses*, Geoffrey Bles, London

Gault, S. Millar and Synge, Patrick M. (1971) *The Dictionary of Roses in Colour*, Ebury Press and Michael Joseph, London

Harkness, Jack (1978) *Roses*, Dent, London

Hole, S. Reynolds (1869) *A Book About Roses*, Blackwood, London

Hollis, Leonard (1971) *Roses*, Hamlyn, London

Hurst, Dr C. C. (1941) *Notes on the Origin and Evolution of Our Garden Roses*, Royal Horticultural Society, London

Kordes, Wilhelm (1965) *Roses* (English Edition), Studio Vista, London

Le Grice, Edward B. (1965) *Rose Growing Complete*, Faber, London

McFarland, Dr J. Horace (1969) *Modern Roses 7*, McFarland, Harrisburgh Pa., USA

Paul, William (1848) *The Rose Garden*, Kent, London

Shepherd, Roy E. (1954) *History of the Rose*, Macmillan, New York

Thomas, Graham Stuart (1955) *The Old Shrub Roses*, Phoenix House, London

Thomas, Graham Stuart (1962) *Shrub Roses of Today*, Phoenix House, London

Thomas, Graham Stuart (1965) *Climbing Roses Old and New*, St Martins, London

Willmott, Ellen (1910) *The Genus Rosa*, Murray, London

Wylie, Ann P. (1954–5) *The History of Garden Roses*, Journal of the Royal Horticultural Society, London

How to Grow Good Roses

Roses are among the easiest of garden plants to grow and maintain. However, a poorly looked after plant will soon show signs of neglect. Roses will thrive on almost all soils from light greensands to moderate clays. They will, of course, do best on rich loam – as all plants – but it is not essential for the production of fine specimens, even to top exhibiting standards. This does not mean that Roses will thrive in any part of the garden just because you would like to see them there, They hate draughts, not, I hasten to say, windy situations. A funnel-effect caused by buildings or by some types of terrain will create an almost impossible situation for any plant to thrive.

Feeding

Adequate nourishment is essential for Roses to grow well and, in growing well, produce an abundance of bloom. The best time to apply food is after spring pruning, and at the early production of spring and summer growth. There is no point in encouraging soft autumnal growth which will not flower and will eventually be damaged by frost to the extent of requiring removal by pruning. Almost all soils need the replenishment of humus, best applied in the form of well-rotted farmyard manure or garden compost, or one of the many peat-based products offered at shops and garden centres. Organic feeds such as bone meal are also beneficial. Having applied any of these after spring pruning, the use of a proprietary Rose fertilizer is to be recommended in late spring or early summer.

When preparing the garden before planting, care should be taken that the site is well drained. Roses dislike cold, boggy soil. Double-digging is an excellent idea if it can be done, but care must be taken that in shallow soils the subsoil is not brought to the surface. When replacing Roses in existing beds, it is essential to remember that without removing the immediate soil and replacing it from a part of the garden which has not previously grown Roses, disappointment will inevitably ensue. Transplant diseases and die-back are sure to result.

Planting

Traditionally the transplanting season is during the period of dormancy (i.e., roughly between November and March in the British Isles). In some places, plants may be purchased earlier, a practice deprecated by the writer who feels that commerce is here taking precedence over the wants of the plants. Many nurseries and garden centres offer Roses in containers. This refers to the practice of extending the planting season by potting up in a peat and sand mix in plastic sleeves, or in some countries in metal cans, which means that the season can carry on after dormancy is broken, usually until early summer. That they should be planted by this time can be seen by the state of plants still offered in late summer. One day perhaps techniques may be developed to enable first-quality plants to be available in containers throughout the year.

If bare-root Roses are received during inclement weather and the ground is obviously unfit for planting, they should be heeled in (or trenched in). The same applies if the planting site is not ready, or if you just do not have the time to deal with the trees properly.

There are a great many planting aids on the market, almost all are peat based. A completely satisfactory planting mixture can be made by adding a large handful of sterilised bone meal to a 2 gallon (10 litre) bucketful of moist horticultural peat, medium grade, often sold as shrub or Rose peat. A double handful of this mixture should be placed at the bottom of the hole dug out to receive the plant. The hole should be at least big enough to be able to spread the roots out. It will be appreciated that most budded Rose plants are developed on one side more than the other and it is useful to remember that if positioned facing away from the source of light, a more balanced plant will develop eventually.

Most modern hybrid Roses, and this includes all Hybrid Teas, Floribundas and their derivative Climbers, having lost the ability to direct their growth without pruning, need help to produce both the quantity and the quality of bloom and foliage towards which Rose breeders have aimed. Both correct pruning and correct feeding are directed towards this end.

Pruning

A newly purchased bare-root Rose will have been trimmed to ensure neat packing, it will not have been pruned (unless it has been purchased at the end of the season as a pruned plant). Hybrid Teas and Floribundas, either in bush or standard (tree) form, must be pruned just before the end of the period of dormancy, i.e. before the sap starts to rise and the early spring growth commences. This can only be determined by observation and it is a foolhardy person who lays down the law by quoting calendar dates. The first part of any pruning operation, whether the subject be a Hybrid Tea, Floribunda, Climber or Shrub Rose, is the removal of any twiggy, distorted, spindly growth, and in the case of old plants, the removal of old and/or decaying stumps which may have accumulated. After this has been done, it is an easy matter to shorten the main shoots. In a newly-planted bush Rose, this will leave the plant about 4–6 in (10–15 cm) in height. Bearing in mind that this is carried out year after year, it is obvious that an aged Rose will gradually attain a greater height after pruning unless a fortuitous crop of main shoots start from ground level. On occasions we may be faced with gnarled old specimens which have been maltreated for years, it being obvious that any new growth will start from about 3 ft (1 m) above the ground level. In this case pruning should take place in complete dormancy (say in mid-winter) and the cuts made way down in the old wood. In this way a rough-growing ancient monster can be reduced to a spritely-looking plant quite easily.

A good pair of sharp secateurs or a knife should be used on manageable wood. Of course if thick old growth is to be dealt with, a pruning saw is necessary. It must be remembered that bruised tissues invite the invasion of harmful bacteria, and secateurs with two sharp cutting blades are preferable to the anvil type. Another cardinal rule is that any cuts made should be about $\frac{1}{4}$ in (6 mm) above a potential new growth (a bud) and that the cut be made on a slope so that rain drops run off and do not remain to create a reservoir for harmful decay-forming bacteria to proliferate. The trouble called by many 'die-back' is quite often attributable to this.

While talking about die-back and pruning, it should be mentioned that any unripe wood left from the previous autumn may be a cause of this trouble and any such wood must be removed along with the first tidying up before pruning the main shoots.

Climbers and Ramblers are usually pruned and tied back in the autumn, before winter storms can cause damage to young growths which are not given adequate support. Ramblers, which produce young basal growths after their short summer flowering is over, may be drastically treated by complete removal of old flowering shoots and the tying-in of the current year's growth to replace them in the flowering season.

The older Climbing Roses (those labelled with the prefix Cli.), require a special treatment of their own. The main shoots which are produced sparingly must not be removed unless there be a replacement to take over, and the lateral shoots need shortening back to an eye or two, about 2 in (5 cm) from the main stem. There are a few climbers, such as 'Mermaid' and the 'Banksian Roses' which are not pruned to promote flower. Their bloom is produced on previous year's lateral and sub-lateral growth, so it is obvious that anything more than a light tidy-up would be too drastic.

Diseases and Pests

When opening a gardening paper, one is invariably assailed by advertisements of the chemical companies giving the impression that the Rose is a constant victim of a multitude of pests and diseases – not intentionally, I am sure, for they do after all want to sell their products. However, as a Rose grower, I must assure you that provided the Rose is well fed, pruned correctly, and grown in the right environment, three-quarters of the battle against most enemies of the Rose has been won. If, however, climatic conditions are on the side of the more common pests and diseases, then be comforted by the thought that the aforesaid chemical companies are ready to come to your aid. Greenfly, thrips and leaf-rolling sawfly are the main pests which attack the Rose in early summer, and while they are certainly not deadly, they can cause unsightly growth-distortion.

Mildew is the whitish-grey film which appears on leaves, usually in late summer and autumn. It can respond to a contact spray, but as with the other Rose pests and diseases, the newer systemic sprays can be so efficacious that a regular spray with a 'cocktail' of compatible compounds is to be recommended on the appearance of any trouble.

Black Spot, the most disfiguring disease of all, can also be treated with one of these systemics. This is neither the time nor place to name specific brands of sprays because diseases can become resistant to a particular formula, and for this reason a change of treatment can be a good plan. Also, modern research is continuously producing better ways of combatting the ills which may beset the garden.

The Classification of Roses Recommended by the World Federation of Rose Societies

Modern Garden Roses

Roses of hybrid origin not bearing any strong resemblance to wild roses (species) and not included in classifications in general use before the introduction of Hybrid Tea Roses.

Non-Climbing

Plants with self-supporting stems.

Non-Recurrent Flowering
Flowering season limited, in spring or summer with at best only occasional blooms in the autumn.
> *Shrub* Plants usually taller and/or possibly wider than Bush Roses and particularly suitable for use as specimen plants.

Recurrent Flowering
Flowering season long or with a marked resurgence later.
> *Shrub* Plants usually taller and/or possibly wider than Bush Roses and particularly suitable for use as specimen plants.
> *Bush* Varieties of moderate height particularly suitable for cultivation in groups:
>> *Large Flowered (Hybrid Tea)* Roses usually having flowers of medium to large size, (petals of double and semi-double varieties overlapped to form a conical, ovoid or other symmetrical centre and those of single varieties large and forming a shapely bud) and capable of being cut as an individual flower (with or without side buds) on a long stem.
>> *Clustered Flowered (Floribunda)* Roses distinguished primarily by a mass of flowers produced in trusses, clusters or on many stems. The flowers may be single, semi-double or double.
>> *Polyantha* Roses with small flowers, usually of rosette form, borne in large clusters. Distinctive foliage, the leaflets smaller than those of Cluster Flowered roses.
>> *Miniature* Roses with miniature flowers, foliage and growth.

Climbing

Plants climbing or rambling with long sprawling or arching stems normally requiring support.

Non-Recurrent Flowering
Flowering season limited, in spring or summer with at best only occasional blooms in the autumn.
> *Rambler* Climbing Roses with lax stems.
> *Climber* Climbing Roses with stiffer stems than Ramblers.
> *Climbing Miniature* Climbing Roses with very small flowers and foliage.

Recurrent Flowering
Flowering season long or with a marked resurgence later.
> *Rambler*   Climbing Roses with lax stems.
> *Climber*   Climbing Roses with stiffer stems than Ramblers.
> *Climbing Miniature*   Climbing Roses with very small flowers and foliage.

   Each ultimate class may be further divided into double, semi-double and single flowered as follows:
> *Double* – varieties which normally have more than twenty petals.
> *Semi-double* – varieties which normally have eight to twenty petals.
> *Single* – varieties which normally have fewer than eight petals.

Old Garden Roses

Roses already well established in classifications in common use before the introduction of Hybrid Tea Roses. (These old classes were based largely on presumed genetical and botanical affinities and in general do not fit easily into a modern classification based mainly on functional garden qualities).

Non-Climbing

Plants with self-supporting stems.

> **Alba**   Roses displaying the influence of *Rosa alba*.

> **Bourbon**   Roses displaying the influence of *Rosa × bourboniana*, supposedly a hybrid between the China Rose and Autumn Damask.

> **Boursault**   Roses supposedly displaying the influence of *Rosa chinensis* and *Rosa pendulina*.

> **China**   Roses displaying the influence of *Rosa chinensis*.

> **Damask**   Roses displaying the influence of *Rosa damascena*.

> **Gallica**   Roses displaying the influence of *Rosa gallica*.

> **Hybrid Perpetual**   Roses usually obtained by inter-breeding Bourbon roses with China and/or Damask Roses.

> **Moss**   Roses with mossy outgrowth on sepals and/or pedicels.

> **Portland**   Roses allied to 'Duchess of Portland' a hybrid suggesting the influence of China and Damask Roses.

> **Provence** (Centifolia)   Roses displaying the influence of *Rosa centifolia*.

Sweet Briar   Roses displaying the influence of *Rosa eglanteria.*

Tea   Roses displaying the influence of *Rosa* × odorata, supposedly a hybrid between *Rosa chinensis* and *Rosa gigantea.*

Climbing

Plants climbing or rambling with long sprawling or arching stems normally requiring support.

Ayrshire   Roses displaying the influence of *Rosa arvensis.*

Boursault   Roses supposedly desplaying the influence of *Rosa chinensis* and *Rosa pendulina.*

Climbing Tea   Climbing Roses with flowers similar to those of Tea Roses.

Noisette   Roses displaying the influence of *Rosa* × *noisettiana*, supposedly a hybrid between *Rosa chinensis* and *Rosa moschata.*

Sempervirens   Roses displaying the influence of *Rosa sempervirens.*

Wild Roses

Species and their varieties or hybrids (single or double flowered) which bear a strong resemblance to species.

Non-Climbing

Plants with self supporting stems.

Climbing

Plants climbing or rambling with long sprawling or arching stems normally requiring support.

Rose Classification Chart

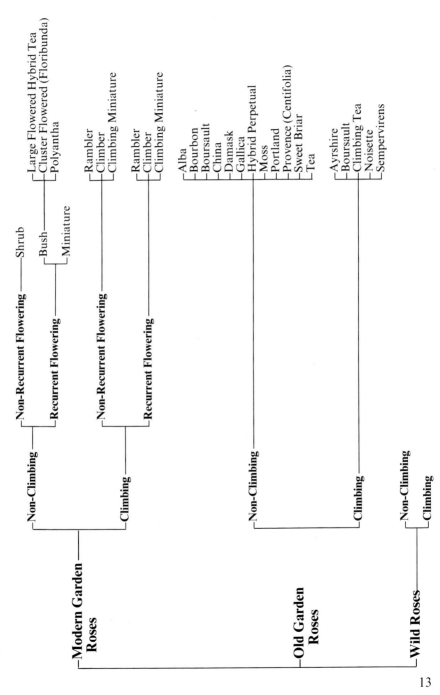

Modern Garden Roses

- **Non-Climbing**
  - **Non-Recurrent Flowering** —— Shrub
  - **Recurrent Flowering**
    - Bush
      - Large Flowered Hybrid Tea
      - Cluster Flowered (Floribunda)
      - Polyantha
    - Miniature
- **Climbing**
  - **Non-Recurrent Flowering**
    - Rambler
    - Climber
    - Climbing Miniature
  - **Recurrent Flowering**
    - Rambler
    - Climber
    - Climbing Miniature

Old Garden Roses

- **Non-Climbing**
  - Alba
  - Bourbon
  - Boursault
  - China
  - Damask
  - Gallica
  - Hybrid Perpetual
  - Moss
  - Portland
  - Provence (Centifolia)
  - Sweet Briar
  - Tea
- **Climbing**
  - Ayrshire
  - Boursault
  - Climbing Tea
  - Noisette
  - Sempervirens

Wild Roses

- **Non-Climbing**
- **Climbing**

Hybridisers of Modern Roses

Under the details of the more recent introductions in this book, the raiser is listed merely under a surname to avoid constant repetition. To many, it is of interest to know where a Rose originates and the following details may be useful:

Armstrong   Armstrong Nurseries, Ontario, California 91761, USA

Bees Ltd   Sealand Nurseries, Chester, England

Cant   Cants of Colchester, The Old Rose Gardens, London Road, Stanway, Colchester, Essex, England

Cocker   James Cocker & Sons, Lang Stracht, Aberdeen, Scotland

Delbard-Chabert   Georges Delbard, 16 Quai de la Megisserie, Paris, France

de Ruiter   G. de Ruiter, Hazerswoude, Holland

Dickson   Alex Dickson succeeded by Patrick Dickson, Dicksons Nurseries Ltd, Newtownards, Co. Down, Northern Ireland

Dot   Simon Dot, San Feliu de Llobregat, Barcelona, Spain

Fryers   Fryers Nurseries Ltd, Manchester Road, Knutsford, Cheshire, England

Gaujard   Jean Gaujard, Feyzin, Isère, France

Gregory   C. Gregory and Son Ltd, Rose Gardens, Stapleford, Nottingham, England

Harkness   Harkness New Roses Ltd, The Rose Gardens, Hitchin, Herts., England

Jackson & Perkins   Jackson and Perkins Co., Medford, Oregon 97501, USA

Kordes   W. Kordes Sohne, 2201 Sparrieshoop, bie Elmshorn, Holstein, West Germany

LeGrice   E. B. LeGrice (Hybridisers) Ltd, Roseland Nurseries, North, Walsham, Norfolk, England

Lens   Pépinières Louis Lens, Wauve-Notre-Dame, Belgium

Mattock   John Mattock Ltd, The Rose Nurseries, Nuneham Courtenay, Oxford, England

McGredy   Sam McGredy Roses International, P.O. Box 14-100, Panmure, Auckland, New Zealand

Meilland   See Universal Rose Selection

Moore   Ralph S. Moore, Sequoia Nurseries, 2519E Noble Avenue, Visalia, California, USA

Poulsen   D. T. Poulsens Planteskole ApS, Kellerisvej 58, 3490 Kvistgaard, Denmark

Tantau   Math. Tantau, Uetersen, Holstein, West Germany

Universal Rose Selection   Meilland et Cie., 06601 Cap d'Antibes, France

World Federation of Rose Societies

'The objects of the Federation, membership of which is open to all Rose Societies representing their countries, are:

To encourage and facilitate the information about and knowledge of 'The Rose' between national Rose societies.

To coordinate the holding of international conventions and exhibitions.

To encourage and, where appropriate, sponsor research into problems concerning the Rose.

To establish common standards for judging new seedling Roses.

To assist in coordinating the registration of Rose names.

To establish a uniform system of Rose classification.

To grant international honours and/or awards.

To encourage and advance international cooperation on all other matters concerning the Rose.'

An effort to achieve these aims would be a great step forward in righting many of the discrepancies which the author has found during his researches towards the writing of this book.

Rose Societies of the World

Argentina: Rose Society of Argentina, Santa Clara, 173, San Isidro 1642, Buenos Aires   **Australia:** The National Rose Society of Australia, 2718 Belmore Road, North Balwyn, Victoria 3104   **Belgium:** Société Royal Nationale les Amis de la Rose, Chateau de L'ast, Mullemhouse, Oost, Vlanderen   **Bermuda:** Bermuda Rose Society, P.O. Box 162, Paget   **Britain:** The Royal National Rose Society, Chiswell Green Lane, St Albans, Hertfordshire AL2 3NR   **Canada:** The Canadian Rose Society, 12 Castlegrove Boulevard, Apartment 18, Don Mills, Ontario M3A 1K8   **Czechoslovakia:** Rosa Club C.S.S.R., R.R., S.N.B., 5, Praha 10   **France:** La Société Française des Roses, Parc de la Tête-d'or, 69459 Lyon   **Germany:** Verein Deutscher, Rosenfreunde, 7570 Baden-Baden, Postfach 1011   **India:** The Rose Society of India, A 267 Defence Colony, New Delhi 110024   **Ireland, Northern:** The Rose Society of Northern Ireland, c/o Fernhill House, Glencairn Park, Glencairn Road, Belfast BT13 3PT   **Israel:** The Israel Rose Society, Ganoth Hadar, P.O. Natania   **Italy:** Associazone Italiano Della Rosa, Villa Reale, 20052, Monza   **Japan:** The Japan Rose Society, 4-12-6 Todoroki Setagayaki, Tokyo   **New Zealand:** The National Rose Society of New Zealand, P.O. Box 9241, Wellington   **Poland:** Polish Rose Society, Browiewskiego 19 M7, Warszawa   **South Africa:** The Rose Society of South Africa, P.O. Box 65217, Benmore, Transvaal 2010   **Switzerland:** Gesellschaft, Schweizerischer, Rosenfreunde, 8158 Regensberg   **United States of America:** The American Rose Society, P.O. Box 30000, Shreveport, Louisiana 71130.

Roses throughout the World

The travels of the genus *Rosa* were not completed when collectors in earlier ages brought back to their patrons' gardens and to an eager public specimens of Roses from far off lands. Having been collected in centres of civilisation in Europe and Asia by military, mercenary and diplomatic expeditions, further distribution was aided by migrations of peoples settling and colonising in previously undeveloped territories. Time and time again, when the distribution of a particular cultivar or species is researched, the records show a fascination with the Rose which is spread far and wide through the world, and the section which follows shows this most clearly.

Britain

The Rose, being so intricately woven into the history and legends of Britain, it is no surprise that it is a national emblem and holds an important place in heraldry.

The climate is particularly suited to the culture of the Rose, the long spring and slow build up to summer produces the necessary sturdy young growth. When summer finally arrives in June and July, the Rose garden is at its peak of perfection. Wherever the Rosarian goes, there are Rose gardens to visit. The famous stately homes throughout the country are often open to the public and Roses are featured in their spectacular gardens. Many are owned by the National Trust (information about the opening of these Trust gardens is available from The National Trust at 43 Queen Anne's Gate, London SW1H 9AS). Other gardens are open to the public under The National Gardens Scheme and are listed in 'Gardens of England and Wales', copies of which are available at most booksellers. Noteworthy to the Rose-lover is the fine new collection at Mottisfont Abbey at Romsey in Hampshire and the gardens at Hidcote in Gloucestershire and at Sissinghurst in Kent.

The Royal National Rose Society, whose headquarters are at Chiswell Green, St Albans in Hertfordshire, was founded in 1876. The first step towards its institution was the arranging of a National Rose Show in July 1858. It was undoubtedly popular, for by 1860 the attendance had risen to 16,000 and the foundation stones towards the National Society had been well and truly laid. In its early days the Society was mainly concerned with organising the Shows, and by the early 1900's the programme had been expanded to include an autumn show as well as a summer show, both held in London, and in more recent times a yearly show held outside London.

In 1937 the first Trial Ground was started at Haywards Heath, later to be removed to Oaklands near St Albans in Hertfordshire, and now at the Chiswell Green headquarters. Here new seedling varieties are tested, not only for the attraction of the flowers, but for health and style of growth. Now instead of new Roses being given awards as specimen blooms on the show bench, the Trial Ground Certificate was a prerequisite to a variety being considered for a Certificate of Merit or the much-coveted Gold Medal.

In 1952 the Society instituted The President's International Trophy to be awarded to the variety considered to be the Best New Seedling Rose of the Year.

The Gardens of the Society's headquarters at St Albans are the Mecca for every Rose lover for here are to be found Roses of every type and description, and of course the now famous Trial Grounds. *The Princess Mary Rose Walk is illustrated opposite.*

16

▲ Gardens of the Royal National Rose Society.

As well as having these magnificent trial grounds at St Albans, the Royal National Rose Society is the organiser of a series of test gardens throughout the United Kingdom. These are to be found in Cardiff in Wales, Edinburgh and Glasgow in Scotland, Harrogate in Yorkshire, Norwich in Norfolk, Nottingham, Redcar in Cleveland, Southport in Merseyside, and Taunton in Somerset.

The Society's gardens at St Albans are the venue of a Festival held each year in July when one can stroll through the gardens at their best, see the magnificent displays of Roses staged by British Rose Nurserymen. You are invited not only to see their Roses, but to talk over your Rose problems (if any) with the experts. Competitions between the amateur Rosarians of Britain show the superb quality of the specimen blooms achieved in gardens throughout the land.

Besides the great park-like gardens, the country has a vast number of surprises, for nowhere else in the world have so many Roses been grown on such small areas as in the front gardens of the ordinary British household, and being so restricted, the true genius of the gardener is seen by the fine mixture of plantings often showing a Rose in new glory by an unusual companion plant.

For the enthusiastic Rosarian searching for new and exciting varieties, or merely looking for a colour to complete a planting scheme, the professional Rose grower is always ready to welcome visitors to show the treasures at his nursery.

▲ The International Rose Trials, Belfast.

Northern Ireland

Small though it may seem when looking at a map of the world, Ulster, or Northern Ireland, has played a very important part in the recent history of the Rose and the names of McGredy, Dickson and Slinger have a great place in the development of the Rose today.

Sam McGredy (the fourth generation Sam that is) has now taken his Rose breeding station to New Zealand (the migration of the know-how and love of the Rose around the globe is what this book is all about) but the Rose still has a great influence in the province.

Patrick Dickson is still breeding Roses in County Down – one of his fine Roses is Grandpa Dickson, which he named in honour of his father, the great Alex Dickson, and his Precious Platinum is one of the best red Hybrid Teas raised to date.

Each year in July an international group of Rosarians gather in Belfast at Sir Thomas and Lady Dixon Park to discuss and to judge Roses which have been growing there for the previous three years. Dixon Park is a magnificent spectacle where acre upon acre of Roses are to be seen at their best. However, in Belfast is also to be found a small public park where the ultimate in Rose culture is to be found. Quite rightly so, for here are trained the parks men of the future. The small Rose garden at Musgrave Park is an absolute gem, the lawns are velvet and each Rose perfection.

19

The Republic of Ireland

In their own quiet way the Irish have built a Rose garden of which to be proud. The Clontarf Horticultural Society could well be called the Irish Rose Society, for at St Annes an enthusiastic body of plantsmen has created, with the cooperation of the Dublin Corporation Parks Department, a broad sweep of a Rose garden. This beautiful park of 266 acres, formerly the home of the Guinness family, is situated close by the sea at Clontarf and imaginatively planted with evergreen oak and pines to provide shelter from the sea winds.

Every type of Rose is represented – old Shrub Roses in great borders, magnificent pergolas and pillars clothed with climbers and ramblers, Hybrid Teas and Floribundas filling 32 beds. The whole garden, when completed, will total some 14,000 Rose trees of all types.

The President of the Society, Leslie Mitchell, and his enthusiastic committee, stage ambitious Rose shows and a yearly competition for the public to join in, an event they call 'Choose Your Rose'. What better way to interest the public in the Rose. No wonder the Irish sing about their favourite flower!

France

To try to single out the most important influence on the Rose in France is well nigh impossible for its history stretched from the Rose garden in Paris created by King Childebert in the first century AD to the great gardens of Bagatelle and of Roseraie de L'Hay.

The modern enthusiasm for the Rose can be said to have started when Napoleon's discarded Empress Josephine, who had retired to Malmaison, started her great collection of Roses which by 1810 numbered about 250 cultivars and species. Associated with Josephine in her collection was the flower painter Redouté, who left a magnificent record in his much-collected works. The influence of André Dupont, who could be described as Josephine's head gardener, was immense, and he soon had many pupils of whom the first was a nurseryman named Descemet who propagated and distributed nearly 300 varieties. He, in turn, had rich patrons and from then on the growth of the Rose was assured. Indeed by 1845, Josephine's collection, which by then had been acquired by the French Government and planted as an exhibition in the Luxemburg Gardens, had grown to 5,000 varieties. Within a century (1950) The Museum of the Rose, The Roseraie de L'Hay, was listing 10,000 varieties.

The great part that French hybridists have played in the development of the Rose as we know it today has been told many times and their names will forever be part of the history of the Rose.

Climbing Roses, Cap d'Antibes. ▶

West Germany

From the days of Salomon Gessner, who found *R. moschata* in a monastery garden in Augsburg in 1565, to the latest seedling from Reimer Kordes at Sparrieshoop, Germany has produced many interesting cultivars in the genus Rosa.

Peter Lambert of Trier showed a remarkable white Rose at the Stutgart Exhibition of 1899 which he named 'Snow Queen'. However, at a later show in Berlin he renamed it 'Frau Karl Druschki'. Classified as a Hybrid Perpetual, it showed influences which had all the marks of a Hybrid Tea, the class which was to oust the Hybrid Perpetuals from their reign as the leading bedding Rose. Peter Lambert also produced another great variety which he named after his home town, 'Trier', a remarkably fragrant shrub Rose with *R. moschata* in its pedigree, and noteworthy as the seedling from which the Rev. Pemberton in England produced the whole range of his famous shrubs which he called, and indeed are still called, the Hybrid Musks.

In the early part of this century, Wilhelm Kordes, a name to become one of the most important in the history of the Rose, having completed his early training in England, returned to Holstein where he joined his brother Hermann in the family business, a business to become one of the largest, if not the largest Rose nursery in Europe. Soon the seedling Roses for which the name Wilhelm Kordes became famous started to appear. His early Hybrid Teas were an immediate success and his 'Geheimrat Duisberg' was for many years the only yellow variety offered by florists. It was also known by its Anglicized name 'Golden Rapture'. It was perhaps his great introduction 'Crimson Glory' which made his reputation.

Not only did Wilhelm produce great Hybrid Teas, but in the 1940's he raised a seedling which was so outstanding that having been accepted by the authorities as a new *species* (albeit a hybrid species), it was given the name of *R. kordesii*, and from it he bred a fine range of Repeat Flowering Shrub and Climbing Roses.

To this day the name of Kordes is synonymous with that of the Rose, for the present head of the family business, Reimer, is also raising great seedlings for the garden of the enthusiastic amateur, for the great parks of the world, and for the florists shops. Like the renowned Wilhelm with his 'Geheimrat Duisberg', Reimer has many cut flower varieties to his credit.

Another name to conjure with is that of Mathias Tantau, raiser of 'Super Star', 'Duke' of Windsor', and 'Fragrant Cloud'.

The German Rose Society, having been cut off from the National Rose Collection (some 6500 varieties) founded in 1903 at Sangerhausen now in East Germany (DDR), decided to make a German National Rosarium at Westfalenpark in Dortmund. In 1969, after the Federal Horticultural Exhibition had closed, the 20 acre gardens were planted, the plans having been commissioned by the Municipality and the Rose Society. It is divided into sections, each representing a different country wherein are collected all the varieties from each hybridist.

'Mercedes', a fine florists' variety. ▶

22

The Netherlands

In researches into the history of the Rose, the name of the Botanical Garden in Leyden figures as a distribution centre as early as the seventeenth century.

Holland may be looked upon not only as a fine distributor of plants, but also of plantsmen. One merely has to look at a list of nurserymen, anywhere in the world and in most countries the influence of The Netherlands is obvious.

Through the list of Roses in cultivation, the names of Spek, Verschuren, Grootendorst, De Vink, de Ruiter are of great importance and influence as Rose breeders and distributors.

The great stock-producing nurseries of north Holland supply a large proportion of the briar understocks for export to other European countries. Each year Rosarians from all over the world gather at the famous Rose garden at The Hague for the International Rose Trials which reach their culmination in mid-July.

Italy

Much of our earliest knowledge about the Rose comes from ancient Rome, where our favourite flower was also held in great esteem. We have seen in earlier pages that the Romans had special houses constructed in order to be able to grow blooms in winter months. The flowers were also used in medicine and in ceremonials; indeed the term *sub rosa* (beneath the rose) still signifies confidentiality today.

The Romans are still greatly attached to the Rose and in their ancient city, set amid mellow ruins, among majestic pines and surrounded by domes and steeples may be found the Rose Garden of Rome, so magnificently described by Stelvio Coggiati in his articles in the Rose Annual of the Royal National Rose Society in the early 1960's. He describes the natural amphitheatre in which the Rose Garden is set and glowingly dwells on the unbroken gallery of two hundred different climbing Roses which crown it, and the imposing collection of four thousand Rose bushes in groups of five of each variety forming an imposing multi-coloured carpet.

Westbroekpark, International Rose Trials, The Hague. ▶

United States of America

To one who lives in a country with recognisable climatic boundaries, the USA presents a bewildering number of zones, ranging from extreme cold to sub-tropical heat and even to arid deserts.

It is easy to see, therefore, that some parts of that vast country are extremely favourable to the culture of the Rose. That is not to say that Roses are grown only in the temperate areas; quite the contrary in fact. It would seem that despite seemingly impossible conditions, the urge to grow the world's favourite flower is just as strong in all parts of the USA as elsewhere.

The most favourable natural climate for Roses is to be found in the western states of Washington and Oregon. However, because the areas of highest population are to be found in New York and California, it is there that the enthusiasm of the Rose gardener reaches its height, despite the high rainfall, coupled with the heat of summer producing ideal conditions for the spread of Black Spot in the eastern states, and the arid desert-like conditions to be found in many western states.

The major commercial production of Rose bushes is to be found in Texas and California where, of course, irrigation is needed. However, the low humidity favours the Rose in its fight against Black Spot.

The nursery industry had an early place in American commerce, although it was little known until the nineteenth century. At Flushing, New York, on Long Island the Prince family opened the first commercial nursery in 1737 and for four generations it was a flourishing concern. Roses were among the many plants listed as growing on their 120 acre nursery.

A landmark in the history of the Rose in the USA was a seedling Rose named for its raiser 'Champney's Pink Cluster.' In 1811 this variety was sent by a Charleston nurseryman, Philippe Noisette, to his brother Louis in Paris. This proved to be a sensation which had far-reaching results on Rose breeding in Europe and originated the group named for its introducer 'Noisettiana', which, as mentioned earlier in this book, had a very strong influence on the development of remontant (repeat flowering) Roses.

From these early stirrings of Rose hybridising in what came to be known as the United States of America has risen an exciting industry which has seen the rise of a whole host of names which figure very prominently in the evolution of the modern Rose. Many of these names will be found in the section on Rose varieties and on hybridists.

Shrub Rose, 'Golden Wings'. ▶

▲ The Rose Garden, Boener Botanical Gardens, Wisconsin.

Canada

Most of the country is too cold for Roses other than the hardiest shrub types and where a few determined Rose lovers do grow them, a great deal of winter protection is needed. The Canadian Rose Society numbers only about one thousand members, understandably so with so few areas suited to Rose cultivation, and those far apart. However, it makes up in enthusiasm what it lacks in size.

There is some experimentation in breeding new varieties and types of Roses. Dr H. Marshall of Morden, Manitoba, the Central Experimental Farm in Ottawa, and Percy H. Wright of Saskatoon, Saskatchewan are all hybridisers working on hardy landscape Roses. Dr F. L. Skinner and Mr G. Buquet have introduced a number of cultivars which are hardy in the Prairies. A long term project at Guelph University to find a typical hardy Canadian Rose is being financed by the Canadian Rose Society and others.

Moves are being made by the Federal Minister of Agriculture to prepare a bill to enact plant breeders' legislation and the Canadian Ornamental Plant Foundation assists originators of plants and organizes distribution.

It can therefore be seen that a lively interest is taken in Roses by the Canadians, and I am grateful to Dr Keith Laver who has kept me informed of the progress of the Rose in Canada.

▲ The International Test Rose Garden, Portland, Oregon.

International Rose Trials

The number of new seedling Roses introduced each year are but a few compared with the great number offered by hybridists from all parts of the world. It is because of this that many of the great Rose Societies hold competitions in order that each variety may be evaluated and its performance may be pointed.

In Britain we have the Trial Grounds of the Royal National Rose Society at St Albans, and in Northern Ireland the Belfast International Rose Trials.

These trials are echoed throughout the world and the awards made, usually headed by a special trophy such as the President's International Trophy for the Best New Seedling Rose of the Year (Britain), The Golden Rose of the Hague (Holland), and The Gold Star of the South Pacific (New Zealand). The Gold Medal heads the list in most countries, followed by Certificates of Merit or Silver Medals, and often special prizes.

Among the principal Rose Trials are:

The All American Rose Selection	France (Bagatelle and at Orleans)
Germany (Baden-Baden)	Italy (Rome and Monza)
Belgium (West Flanders)	Netherlands (The Hague)
Britain (St Albans)	New Zealand (Palmerston North)
Czechoslovakia (Hradec Králové)	Switzerland (Geneva)

▲ The Rose Garden, Johannesburg Botanical Gardens.

Africa

From the shores of the Mediterranean, through deserts, tropical forests, high plains and the coastal regions to the more temperate Cape Peninsula, it is interesting to find and hear of Rose growers, amateur and professional.

Roses have long been grown in Egypt, Morocco and Algeria. Indeed the writer was most interested to find Roses growing in the ruins of the ancient Roman city of Timgad in Algeria, although these are more likely to be survivors of the French settlers rather than from Roman colonial times.

When Ghana was known as the Gold Coast, one heard of the attempts to grow Roses under the most difficult of conditions, but in present times it appears that more success is being found using up-to-date techniques; indeed in several countries through the central zone of Africa, great success has been achieved.

Many Roses have been successfully grown in Kenya. The production of Rose plants commercially was initiated by Closeburn Nurseries and now the Rose is well established.

Ethiopia even has its own Rose species – as far as one can ascertain the only native African Rose. It has been distributed but not grown as an ornamental plant for the garden.

South Africa has a thriving Rose Society and its members have become well known throughout the Rose world by their enthusiastic attendance at the International Rose conferences in recent years. Roses do well in the Cape, on the High Veld, in the Transvaal and even in the humid heat of Natal. However, the colours do tend to be rather less intense than in Europe, but of course the Rose season extends to nine or ten months.

30

▲ Rakir Rose Garden, Chandigar.

India

India is the home of several Species Roses which grow wild, mostly in the mountainous areas of the Himalayan range. The cultivation of Rose gardens was referred to in Sanskrit works. The Moguls were great admirers of the Rose and the Empress Nur Jehan is credited, in legend, with the discovery of Attar of Roses.

The Rose Society of India, founded in 1958 with His Highness Maharaja Yadavindra of Patiala as the founder President, lists its aims as: To disseminate knowledge of the Rose and Rose growing; to encourage, improve and extend the cultivation of the Rose by means of scientific trials; to hold exhibitions and shows; and to organise other activities to further the cause of the Rose.

The first All India Rose Show was organised by the Society in December 1959 in the grounds of the Botany Division of the Indian Agricultural Research Institute, New Delhi. Subsequent shows were held on the same grounds until 1962, after which they were organised at a site subtending the famous Safdarjang Tomb in New Delhi. It was found by experience that while shows held in December were very good in the Hybrid Tea classes, Floribundas were not at their best at this time of the year. A spring Rose Show is therefore held at the end of March when there is maximum bloom in the gardens and the Floribundas are able to be shown at their best.

In the more tropical parts of the country, many of the orange and yellow shades fail to develop their full colours but it is hoped that modern breeding will produce varieties which will overcome this difficulty.

31

▲ Veale Rose Garden, Adelaide.

Australia

The first Rose Society in Australia, the National Rose Society of Victoria, was established in the early part of this century. It was not, however, until the early 1970's that the Australian Rose Society was formed linking the various state societies.

The early settlers in Australia came from Britain and with them they brought the idea of the home garden. Vying with neighbours had led to the formation of Horticultural Societies and the resultant competitions led to the early shows. As in most countries which are hot and dry through the summer with winters comparatively mild and wet, the southern parts of Australia are almost ideal for the enthusiastic Rose growers. The main flush of bloom is borne in late October and early November in Melbourne; in Adelaide and Sydney the bloom is a little earlier; whereas Hobart in Tasmania is two weeks later. The more northerly areas are hotter and wetter and the incidence of Black Spot very high, making the culture of the Rose very difficult.

Most of the varieties grown are the same as grown elsewhere in the world, but because of the heat, those with a higher petallage last longer and are therefore more popular.

▲ Benalla Rose Garden, Victoria.

New Zealand

Once again the challenge of growing Roses in an area less suited to their culture produces the paradox of more Rosarians from what might be termed the sub-tropical north, rather than the cooler climes of the south of the islands which are ideal for the Rose.

The National Rose Society of New Zealand is an enthusiastic body whose members are grouped into District Rose Societies, who each run their own Rose shows with what appears to be a large number of entries.

The Society was host to the International Rose Convention in the city of Hamilton in November 1971 and apart from the shows, visits and lectures enjoyed by over 1,500 delegates from all over the world, the name of Hamilton will be looked upon as a landmark in the folklore of the Rose, for it was here at the 1971 Convention that the World Federation of Rose Societies was inaugurated.

One cannot finish a short note on New Zealand and Roses without mentioning one of the great names in Rose breeding: Sam McGredy. The fourth in a line of Rose growers originating in Portadown, Northern Ireland, he has taken his Rose hybridizing to Panmure, near Auckland from where many exciting new varieties may be expected.

33

Bush Roses of the Hybrid Tea Type

For convenience sake the term Hybrid Tea is now taken to mean all of the large-flowered type of bedding Roses whose flowers, of classic shape, are borne singly, or in well-spaced small clusters. I suppose that it would be fair to say that should one mention the word 'Rose' to many people, their mental picture would be that which an enthusiastic Rosarian would know as a Hybrid Tea.

Strictly speaking the term Hybrid Tea must be considered obsolete. There are few, if any Roses which can be recognised as having a variety of the Tea Rose as a parent. The class originated it is now conjectured, as a cross between the Hybrid Perpetuals and the Tea Roses. The early records imply that the first varieties were selections from sowings of seed gathered from garden plants of a Tea Rose variety. The names of Lacharme, Verdier, Paul and Guillot all figured in the breeding and selection of the early varieties and it was with the introductions by Henry Bennett in 1879 of ten varieties with fully-documented parentages that one could say that the class had 'arrived'.

Since those early days other types and species have been used and in most of today's varieties, a highly-complicated 'family tree' will show other Roses whose characteristics have been thought desirable to add to that of our favourites. Thus we have the introduction of the new colours yellow and orange in the early part of the century; of the new crimsons in the 1930's; and the luminous cinnabar-reds in the 1950's, which in turn gave rise to the brilliant vermilions of the present.

The further a cultivar gets from its parent species, the more important is the care required when pruning, and this is amply illustrated in the case of the Hybrid Tea type of Rose. They regenerate themselves by producing strong basal shoots yearly. In many cultivars this requires assistance by removal of the previous year's growth to enable sap supply to be concentrated on this new growth. Some varieties need quite rigorous pruning each year, while others repay light pruning according to their strength, the effect required, and the climatic conditions prevailing. The same considerations will govern the time of pruning. However, there are certain strict rules which must be followed, to whichever school of thought one belongs, and the most important is that all weak, twiggy shoots must be removed, as should any late growths which are unripe.

'Kronenbourg'. ▶

34

Adolph Horstmann

(illustrated)

Parentage Dr Verhage × Colour Wonder
Raiser Kordes
Year of introduction 1972
Full blooms of medium size and good shape, some fragrance. The colour is deep golden-yellow, edged and shaded pink. The growth is vigorous and upright, the foliage mid-bronze-green and is semi-glossy.

Varieties of similar colour (orange-gold-apricot) not illustrated:

Alpine Sunset

Parentage Dr A. J. Verhage × Grandpa Dickson
Raiser Cant
Year of introduction 1974
Large globular blooms of peach and gold with deep fragrance, the growth is vigorous and upright and the foliage is large, glossy and medium green.

Beaute

Parentage Mme Joseph Perraud × unnamed seedling
Raiser Mallerin
Year of introduction 1953
High-centred blooms of soft orange-apricot, of elegant shape. A fine Rose for the flower arranger. Hardy and healthy in some countries, but in Britain has been found rather soft and frost-prone. It also has shown some susceptibility to Black Spot. Slight fragrance.

Bettina

Parentage Peace × (Mme Joseph Perraud × Demain)
Raiser Meilland
Year of introduction 1953
A vigorous plant with somewhat lush growth, which has a tendency to Black Spot in years when it is prevalent. The medium-sized blooms of bright golden-orange are heavily veined red. Sweet fragrance.

Diorama

Parentage Peace × Beaute
Raiser de Ruiter
Year of introduction 1965
Rich golden-yellow flowers of good high-centred shape, a most elegant flower which stands up well to bad weather. Can sometimes produce exhibition-sized flowers. Medium, upright growth of branching habit. An outstanding variety in this colour range.

Alexander   *(illustrated)*

Parentage   Super Star × (Ann Elizabeth × Allgold)
Raiser   Harkness
Year of introduction   1972
A brilliant vermilion Rose with medium-sized rather thin blooms borne in great profusion, often in clusters, on a tall, upright bush, well-clothed in plentiful glossy foliage. Named for Field Marshal Viscount Alexander of Tunisia.

Varieties of similar colour (vermilion shades) not illustrated:

Duke of Windsor   (synonym Herzog von Windsor)

Parentage   A Prima Ballerina seedling
Raiser   Tantau
Year of introduction   1968
Unusually bright vermilion flowers of medium size and deep fragrance. The large luxuriant dark green foliage is extremely susceptible to mildew.
   Named for H.R.H., The Duke of Windsor, formerly the Prince of Wales and Edward VIII.

Fragrant Cloud   (synonym Duftwolke and Nuage Parfume)

Parentage   Seedling × Prima Ballerina
Raiser   Tantau
Year of introduction   1963
The heavy perfume of this variety is the perfect answer to those who say that modern Roses have no fragrance. Large, well-shaped blooms of coral-scarlet, which mature with a slight crimson hue. Very free-flowering. A vigorous bushy plant with branching growth. Winner of the Royal National Rose Society President's International Trophy 1964.

Kathleen O'Rourke

Parentage   Not known
Raiser   Dickson
Year of introduction   1977
A strong, healthy plant with large leathery foliage. The large blooms of classic shape are of mid-pink with hints of salmon. Named by the raisers at the request of an Australian who wished to give his wife the ultimate in birthday gifts.

Super Star   (synonym Tropicana)

Parentage   (seedling × Peace) × (seedling × Alpine Glow)
Raiser   Tantau
Year of introduction   1960
When introduced, the colour of Super Star caused a sensation. Pure light vermilion blooms of medium size, borne singly and in clusters. The growth is tall and upright and is well-clothed with matt foliage of medium green which may require protection from mildew.

Blue Moon   (synonym Mainzer Fashnacht and Sissi)   (*illustrated*)
Parentage   Unnamed seedling × Sterling Silver
Raiser   Tantau
Year of introduction   1964
Large well-shaped, sweetly scented blooms of silvery lilac. At the moment it is still the best of the so-called blue Roses. Strong healthy foliage, more robust than many of this colour range, though it has been found to be frost-prone.

Varieties of similar colour (lilac-lavender-blue) not illustrated:

Cologne Carnival   (synonyms Kolner Karneval and Blue Girl)
Parentage   Not published
Raiser   Kordes
Year of introduction   1964
Very much like Blue Moon, but without its deliciously sweet fragrance.

Harry Edland
Parentage   (Lilac Charm × Sterling Silver) × [Blue Moon × (Sterling Silver × Africa Star)]
Raiser   Harkness
Year of introduction   1976
Full fragrant blooms of deep lilac mauve, borne freely on a bush of vigorous bushy growth. The foliage is glossy and dark green. Named in memory of a great rosarian sometime Secretary of the Royal National Rose Society.

Intermezzo
Parentage   Grey Pearl × Lila Vedri
Raiser   Dot
Year of introduction   1962
A blue Rose from Spain. Vigorous, bushy growth, but little fragrance. Free flowering. Some Black Spot.

Lilac Time
Parentage   Golden Dawn × Luis Brinas
Raiser   McGredy
Year of introduction   1956
Very fragrant blooms of medium size are of elegant classic shape and of lilac-pink shaded magenta. The foliage is light green, and the growth moderately vigorous.

Sterling Silver
Parentage   Seedling × Peace
Raiser   Fisher
Year of introduction   1958
A cut flower variety of silvery blue which does well under glass but is a trifle thin in growth for garden cultivation. Very fragrant.

40

Chivalry (synonym Macpow) *(illustrated)*

Parentage Unknown
Raiser McGredy
Year of introduction 1977

A tall bush of great vigour. The flamboyant blooms of deep gold and old ivory are deeply shaded at the edges of the petals with Chinese red and are borne on sturdy long stems plentifully clothed with dark green glossy foliage.

Varieties of similar colour (yellow and orange-scarlet blends) not illustrated:

Colour Wonder (synonym Königen der Rosen)

Parentage Perfecta × Super Star
Raiser Kordes
Year of introduction 1964

A bi-colour of orange-salmon and yellow. The full blooms are borne on a bush of moderately short habit with disease-resistant foliage making this a fine bedding Rose.

Gay Gordons

Parentage Belle Blonde × Karl Herbst
Raiser Cocker
Year of introduction 1969

A brilliant bi-colour of red and yellow. Unfortunately it has proved susceptible to Black Spot.

Harry Wheatcroft (synonym Caribia)

Parentage A sport from Piccadilly
Raiser Wheatcroft
Year of introduction 1973

A bizarre bloom streaked and striped scarlet and gold. Named for a great Rosarian.

Piccadilly

Parentage McGredys Yellow × Karl Herbst
Raiser McGredy
Year of introduction 1960

An exciting confection of scarlet and gold, the compact bushy plant is covered with a profusion of scarlet and gold high-pointed buds. The bright shiny disease-resistant foliage amply clothes this fine variety.

Tzigane

Parentage Peace × J. B. Meilland
Raiser Meilland
Year of introduction 1951

Full blooms of scarlet-orange and chrome-yellow borne on an upright bush of moderate vigour. The dark glossy foliage may need protection from mildew in years when it is rife.

Dekorat (synonym Freude) (*illustrated*)

Parentage Not published
Raiser Kordes
Year of introduction 1977
Large, well-shaped blooms of coral-pink shot with tinges of pale gold – at times quite pronounced. The plant is vigorous and of above-average size – it could almost be described as shrubby. Well-clothed with attractive, healthy foliage. Good in almost all situations.

Varieties of similar colour (coral-orange-salmon) not illustrated.

Blessings

Parentage A seedling of The Queen Elizabeth Rose
Raiser Gregory
Year of introduction 1968
Shapely fragrant blooms of delicate orange-salmon, very freely borne, often singly, but sometimes betraying the Floribunda in its ancestry. A sturdy grower of medium height and vigorous upright habit. Strongly recommended as a bedding variety.

Femina

Parentage Fernand Arles × Mignonne
Raiser Gaujard
Year of introduction 1963
A medium sized bloom of coppery salmon which opens to pink, carried on a vigorous bush of erect growth, clothed with semi-glossy foliage which needs some protection from Black Spot in situations (and at times) where it is rife.

Mischief

Parentage Peace × Spartan
Raiser McGredy
Year of introduction 1960
Full well-shaped fragrant blooms of soft coral-salmon. The branching growth is vigorous and is well-clothed with semi-glossy light green foliage which may need protection from rust in areas where this disease is prevalent.

Tenerife

Parentage Fragrant Cloud × Piccadilly
Raiser Bracegirdle
Year of introduction 1972
Large fat blooms of deep coral-salmon, with pale peach-pink reverse. Very fragrant. A tendency to Black Spot mars the glossy, medium green foliage.

Elizabeth Harkness   (*illustrated*)

Parentage   Red Dandy × Piccadilly
Raiser   Harkness
Year of introduction   1968
Large well-shaped blooms of pale creamy buff, lightly shaded pink. Sweetly fragrant. Towards the end of the flowering season, in the autumn, it has a tendency to lose colour and to appear white. Named for the wife of the raiser.

Varieties of similar colour (pale flesh pink shaded buff) not illustrated:

Lakeland

Parentage   Not known
Raiser   Fryer
Year of introduction   1976
Large blooms of soft pearl-pink, a fine exhibition Rose with excellent foliage and habit of growth. Named as a compliment to a distinguished Rose society in England.

Memoriam

Parentage   (Blanche Mallerin × Peace) × (Peace × Frau Karl Druschki)
Raiser   Von Abrams
Year of introduction   1960
Off-white blooms of good shape, tinted pale pink. Good in dry weather, but dislikes rain. A good variety for the exhibitor. Named by the raiser in memory of his wife.

Ophelia

Parentage   Unknown
Raiser   Paul
Year of introduction   1912
Still a firm favourite, whose fragrant well-shaped blooms of medium size bring back memories of the gardens of childhood days. The colour, pale flesh-pink, with a tint of soft yellow at the base of the petals. The early summer flowers are subject to damage by thrips. Named after the sad heroine of Shakespeare's *Hamlet*.

Royal Highness   (synonym Königliche Hoheit)

Parentage   Virgo × Peace
Raiser   Swim
Year of introduction   1962
A very full-flowered, pale pink, high-centred variety which dislikes wet weather. A variety which is excellent for the exhibitor.

Fragrant Hour

(illustrated)

Raiser McGredy
Year of introduction 1973
Salmon-pink blooms of beautiful shape, rich fragrance and good size, borne on a tallish bush of upright habit and attractive foliage.

Varieties of similar colour (peach-salmon-pink) not illustrated:

Bonsoir

Raiser Dickson
Year of introduction 1968
Very full fragrant exhibition blooms of peach-pink. Unfortunately badly marked by wet weather. Vigorous, upright growth. Healthy dark green foliage. Named for its commercial sponsor.

Mme Butterfly

Parentage A sport from Ophelia
Raiser Hill
Year of introduction 1918
A favourite from yesterday's garden. The very fragrant blooms of classic shape are flesh-pink. An excellent variety for cutting. The growth of the plant is still vigorous, but the foliage does not compare well with modern varieties. Some trouble in the early season from thrip, but worth growing for the memories it evokes. The name is of course the heroine of Puccini's great opera.

Sweet Promise (synonyms Sonia, Sonia Meilland)

Parentage Zambra × (Baccara × Message)
Raiser Meilland
Year of introduction 1973
A beautiful well-shaped bloom of pale peach-pink, borne on a vigorous upright bush. An exquisite cut flower variety which is good under hot, dry conditions, but is not at its best with cool, wet weather.

Pink Supreme

Parentage Amor × Peace
Raiser de Ruiter
Year of introduction 1965
Soft rose-pink blooms on long straight stems, light green glossy foliage, a vigorous bush of branching habit. Very fragrant.

Lady Seton

Parentage Ma Perkins × Mischief
Raiser McGredy
Year of introduction 1966
The sweetly fragrant blooms of clear pink have a fine classic shape and are freely produced on a well-shaped bush clothed with plentiful foliage. Named for the doyenne of the flower arranging world, Julia Clements.

Josephine Bruce

Parentage Crimson Glory × Madge Whipp
Raiser Bees
Year of introduction 1949
Blackish crimson with scarlet shading, the petals of Josephine Bruce are crisp and the shape of the bloom is held, but the fragrance is not so apparent until fully blown. The bush tends to make one-sided spreading growth and it is best pruned to an inward-pointing eye. Some mildew.

Varieties of similar colour (crimson velvet) not illustrated:

Crimson Glory

Parentage Catherine Kordes seedling × W. E. Chaplin
Raiser Kordes
Year of introduction 1935
A truly great Rose in its day. Very fragrant blooms of rich dark crimson, liable to discolour rusty brown in autumn blooming. Some mildew. The parent of many fine red Roses.

Mister Lincoln

Parentage Chrysler Imperial × Charles Mallerin
Raiser Swim and Weeks
Year of introduction 1964
Huge sweetly scented blooms of crimson velvet borne on long sturdy stems. The bush is vigorous and upright. Free-flowering. Not so disease prone as so many of this hue. Named for Abraham Lincoln, the sixteenth President of the United States of America.

Papa Meilland

Parentage Chrysler Imperial × Charles Mallerin
Raiser Meilland
Year of introduction 1963
Were it not for the exquisite fragrance and the classic shape of this deep crimson velvet rose, its susceptibility to mildew would have condemned it completely. A Rose which justifies the constant spraying it requires.

John Waterer

Parentage Karl Herbst × (Ethel Sanday × Hannah)
Raiser McGredy
Year of introduction 1976
Large high-pointed crimson blooms of good substance. Good for both garden display and for those wishing to exhibit. Some fragrance, but not of the heaviness usually associated with Roses of this colour. Vigorous, upright growth.

Just Joey *(illustrated)*

Parentage Fragrant Cloud × Dr Verhage
Raiser Cants
Year of introduction 1973

A beautiful colour, and when introduced quite the best. The coppery-orange blooms are veined red and are of medium size, but a bit shapeless. They are borne on a vigorous, upright bush. The foliage is of dark bronze-green, with a slight tendency to mildew. Named by hybridist Roger Pawsey for his wife.

Varieties of similar colour (copper-apricot-orange) not illustrated:

Bronze Masterpiece

Parentage Golden Masterpiece × Kate Smith
Raiser Jackson and Perkins
Year of introduction 1962

Very full high-centred blooms of apricot-orange, an exhibitor's Rose, which can produce huge blooms.

Valencia

Parentage Golden Sun × Chantre
Raiser Kordes
Year of introduction 1967

Very large double high-centred apricot-orange, fragrant blooms. Foliage is glossy and leathery.

Dr Verhage (synonym Golden Wave)

Parentage Tawny Gold × a Baccara seedling
Raiser Verbeek
Year of introduction 1960

Golden yellow blooms, flushed apricot, whose opening petals are frilled and waved, fragrant. A good variety to grow under glass, it responds well to generous treatment. Dislikes cold wet weather.

Gertrud Schweitzer

Parentage Dr Verhage × Colour Wonder
Raiser Kordes
Year of introduction

Orange-salmon to light apricot blooms of moderate fulness, the vigorous upright growth is well-clothed with semi-glossy medium green foliage which is tinted reddish-bronze in the early stages.

Vienna Charm (synonym Wiener Charm)

Parentage Golden Sun × Chantre
Raiser Kordes
Year of introduction 1963

A tall-growing bush, bearing large blooms of bronze-gold. Popular but not winter hardy. Very fragrant.

King's Ransom (*illustrated*)

Parentage   Golden Masterpiece × Lydia
Raiser   Morey
Year of introduction   1961
Full, well-shaped flower of medium size and of rich, pure yellow. One of the best pure yellow Hybrid Teas. The growth is compact and the dark green foliage is most disease resistant.

Varieties of similar colour (clear bright yellow) not illustrated:

Gold Crown   (synonyms Goldkrone, Corona de Oro, Couroune d'Or)

Parentage   Peace × Spek's Yellow
Raiser   Kordes
Year of introduction   1960
Large, very deep yellow blooms with good fragrance, the vigorous tall, upright growth is extremely strong even to the extent of appearing coarse. The foliage is semi-glossy and dark green.

McGredy's Yellow

Parentage   Mrs Charles Lamplough × (The Queen Alexandra Rose × J. B. Clark)
Raiser   McGredy
Year of introduction   1933
A fine old Rose with many admirers. The clear primrose flowers are of good form and the colour contrasts well with the rich dark reddish brown stems and dark green foliage.

Miss Harp   (synonym Oregold)

Parentage   Piccadilly × Colour Wonder
Raiser   Tantau
Year of introduction   1970
Deep yellow blooms with bronze shades. Tall, vigorous growth. Dark, glossy green foliage.

Spek's Yellow   (synonym Golden Scepter)

Parentage   Golden Rapture × unnamed seedling
Raiser   Verschuren-Pechtold
Year of introduction   1950
High centred, deep yellow bloom of medium size. Some fragrance. Vigorous, upright though somewhat spiky growth. Very free bloom.

Sunblest

Parentage   Unknown
Raiser   Tantau
Year of introduction   1970
Unfading golden-yellow blooms. A tall, upright grower with slight fragrance.

Korp   (synonym Prominent)   (*illustrated*)

Parentage   A Zorina seedling
Raiser   Kordes
Year of introduction   1971
Introduced as a cut flower variety, the neatness of the small flowers is enhanced by the brilliant colour of pure vermilion. The plant is very hardy, healthy and vigorous. It has gone to the top as a garden-worthy variety.

Varieties of similar colour (brightest vermilion) not illustrated:

Coalite Flame

Parentage   Not published
Raiser   Dickson
Year of introduction   1974
Large, high-pointed fragrant flowers of deep glowing vermilion. A vigorous upright grower with large foliage. A commercially sponsored variety.

Fritz Thiedemann

Parentage   Horstmann's Jubiläumrose seedling × Alpine Glow seedling
Raiser   Tantau
Year of introduction   1959
A well-shaped fragrant large bloom of brick red, a bushy grower well-clothed with dark green foliage. Eclipsed by Super Star, its contemporary.

Princess

Parentage   (Peace × Magicienne) × (Independence × Radar)
Raiser   Laperriere
Year of introduction   1964
Clear light vermilion blooms of exhibition size. It dislikes wet weather. Sturdy, short growth.

Summer Holiday

Parentage   A Super Star seedling
Raiser   Gregory
Year of introduction   1968
A big orange-red Rose borne on a somewhat spreading bush. Makes a fine large bush, but rather unwieldy for the average garden.

Mullard Jubilee   (synonym Electron)   (*illustrated*)

Parentage   Paddy McGredy × Prima Ballerina
Raiser   McGredy
Year of introduction   1970
Large fragrant blooms of rose-pink of an unusual brilliance, borne on a robust bushy plant, sometimes singly, and often in clusters. Named for its commercial sponsor's anniversary.

Varieties of similar colour (deep rose-pink) not illustrated:

Mala Rubinstein

Parentage   Not published
Raiser   Dickson
Year of introduction   1971
A very fragrant bloom of deep rose-pink, very good cropping. A vigorous Rose which has won many awards. Named for a commercial sponsor.

Pink Peace

Parentage   (Peace × Monique) × (Peace × Mrs John Laing)
Raiser   Meilland
Year of introduction   1961
Large, full, loosely formed blooms of deep pink, scarcely resembling Peace. The name has counted against this variety by disappointing those gardeners who have expected a replica of that famous Rose in pink.

Prima Ballerina   (synonym Première Ballerina)

Parentage   Unknown seedling × Peace
Raiser   Tantau
Year of introduction   1957
Well-shaped blooms of deep rose-pink with a very deep fragrance, it is one of the parents of Fragrant Cloud. The plant is vigorous and of medium height, the foliage is strong, dark green with a slight tendency to mildew.

Wendy Cussons

Parentage   Not published
Raiser   Gregory
Year of introduction   1959
A Rose distinguished by its very deep fragrance, likened by many to that of the old Damask Roses. The shape of the bloom is good, with attractive, reflexing petals. The plant is vigorous and rather spreading in habit. Named for a member of the family famous for its Imperial Leather toilet preparations.

National Trust (*illustrated*)

Parentage   Evelyn Fison × King of Hearts
Raiser   McGredy
Year of introduction   1970

An excellent bedding Rose with perfectly shaped blooms of deep crimson-scarlet, but alas, no fragrance. The neat, compact bush is vigorous and well-clothed with strong, healthy foliage which is coppery-red when young. Introduced to support its namesake in the year of its introduction.

Varieties of similar colour (crimson-scarlet) not illustrated:

Alec's Red

Parentage   Fragrant Cloud × Dame de Couer
Raiser   Cocker
Year of introduction   1970

Deep red, large well-formed flowers, borne on strong, upright stems. Rich, sweet perfume. A sturdy bush of medium height. For its years in the trials of the Royal National Rose Society it was known merely as Alec's red. When it was introduced, no better name could be found than that to honour its raiser, Alec Cocker.

Big Chief

Parentage   Ernest H. Morse × Red Planet
Raiser   Dickson
Year of introduction   1975

Huge flowers of bright crimson, a good exhibition variety which is excellent in hot summers but dislikes wet weather. An upright grower with large leathery foliage.

Ernest H. Morse

Parentage   Not published
Raiser   Kordes
Year of introduction   1965

A large bright red bloom with sweet fragrance and sturdy upright habit. Ernest Morse, the famous Rosarian, was a great family friend of the raiser.

Karl Herbst

Parentage   Peace × Independence
Raiser   Kordes
Year of introduction   1949

A very vigorous variety which produces full, well-shaped blooms of dull crimson. Fine for exhibition, but liable to be spoiled by wet weather.

Red Devil

Parentage   Silver Lining × Prima Ballerina
Raiser   Dickson
Year of introduction   1967

An enormous bloom of light crimson with a paler reverse on a vigorous upright bush. Good for exhibition, fragrant, but dislikes wet weather. Named by the raiser to honour the 'Red Devils', the parachute regiment.

Pascali *(illustrated)*

Parentage   The Queen Elizabeth Rose × White Butterfly
Raiser   Lens
Year of introduction   1963
Creamy white blooms of good form and substance, stands wet weather better than most whites and is very free-flowering. Quite the best white Hybrid Tea to date, it has dark green foliage, borne on a vigorous upright bush.

Varieties of similar colour (white) not illustrated:

Evening Star

Parentage   Not published
Raiser   Jackson and Perkins
Year of introduction   1977
A large beautifully formed white Hybrid Tea from America which can produce several long-lasting blooms per stem. A sturdy variety of medium-tall growth.

Frau Karl Druschki   (synonym Snow Queen)

Parentage   Marveille de Lyon × Mme Caroline Testout
Raiser   Lambert
Year of introduction   1900
A famous old Rose classified by some as a Hybrid Perpetual. The young flower buds are often splashed crimson, but the developing flower is of pure paper-white, high-pointed and well-shaped. It does, however, suffer badly in wet weather when it has a tendency to balling.

Message   (synonym White Knight)

Parentage   Virgo × Peace
Raiser   Meilland
Year of introduction   1956
A white Rose worth remembering for the flower arrangers, to whom the greenish tinge appeals. Not very free in flower production, its tendency to mildew has served to lose the popularity it had.

Virgo

Parentage   Blanche Mallerin × Neige Parfum
Raiser   Mallerin
Year of introduction   1947
An elegant bloom of pure white, slight fragrance and sparse foliage which is susceptible to mildew, a fault which has spoiled its record.

Peace   (synonyms Gioia, Gloria Dei and Mme A. Meilland) (*illustrated*)

Parentage   [(George Dickson × Souv. de Claudius Pernet) × (Joanna Hall × Charles P. Kilham)] × Margaret McGredy
Raiser   Meilland
Year of introduction   1945
Large fat blooms of bright yellow splashed bright pink which open to enormous flowers of creamy yellow, ruffle-edged and shaded light pink, carried on sturdy smooth stems. The tall wide bushes are a mass of dark green, large, leathery foliage.

Varieties of similar colour (yellow with peach-pink shading) not illustrated:

Chicago Peace

Parentage   A sport of Peace
Discoverer   Johnston
Year of introduction   1962
The deep phlox-pink heavy shading on this sport (mutation) of Peace gives ample reason for its selection. Unfortunately, the colouration is rather unstable, otherwise it is a fine form.

Grand'mere Jenny

Parentage   Peace × Signora
Raiser   Meilland
Year of introduction   1955
A refined 'Peace' with slender buds of pink, peach and yellow. Very free-flowering, though not so robust as its illustrious parent.

Grandpa Dickson

Parentage   (Perfecta × Governador Bragada da Cruz) × Piccadilly
Raiser   Dickson
Year of introduction   1966
Cool lemon-yellow blooms of classic shape and exhibition size. Light green foliage on a bush of moderate upright habit. The blooms betray 'Peace' among its ancestry by the slight blush in the latter part of the season. Patrick Dickson, the raiser, could think of no greater honour he could pay his father, Alex Dickson, a great Rosarian of his day. Winner of the Royal National Rose Society President's Trophy in 1965.

Kronenbourg   (synonym Flaming Peace)

Parentage   Peace sport
Discoverer   McGredy
Year of introduction   1966
A flamboyant sport (mutation) discovered in the rosefields of Northern Ireland. The enormous buds of crimson and gold fade to the plum and ivory blooms beloved by the flower arranger.

Peer Gynt

(*illustrated*)

Parentage Golden Wonder × Golden Giant
Raiser Kordes
Year of introduction 1968
Big plants bearing full yellow blooms which are slightly shaded peach as they age in the hot sun. Very free flowering, often in clusters. The dark green foliage may suffer from mildew where it is prevalent. Named after the hero of Ibsen's folk drama.

Varieties of similar colour (bright yellow, shaded flushed-pink) not illustrated:

Dorothy Peach

Parentage Lydia × Peace
Raiser Robinson
Year of introduction 1957
High centred fragrant blooms of good size, freely borne, deep yellow, flushed pink; the low bushy growth is glossy and dark green.

Mr Chips

Parentage Grandpa Dickson × Miss Ireland
Raiser Dickson
Year of introduction 1970
Large double, high-pointed blooms of soft deep gold with red veinings. The petals are edged and shaded deep cerise. Glossy mid-green foliage.

Yellow Pages

Parentage Arthur Bell × Peer Gynt
Raiser McGredy
Year of introduction 1973
Golden yellow, full flowers with pale pink flush on the edge of the petals. Very freely borne singly, and often several together in small clusters. The upright habit of the bush, the smooth almost thornless stems and glossy light green foliage add to the attraction of this fine bedding Rose. Named for a commercial sponsor.

Young Quinn

Parentage An Arthur Bell seedling
Raiser McGredy
Year of introduction 1976
Large yellow blooms, often showing a trace of 'Peace' in its ancestry by the flush of pink at the edge of the petals. The bush is tall and vigorous and the blooms are especially fine in the autumn. Sam McGredy named this Rose in honour of a famous Trans-Tasman racehorse.

Precious Platinum

(*illustrated*)

Parentage Red Planet × Franklin Engelmann
Raiser Dickson
Year of introduction 1974
One of the best bright crimson-red Hybrid Teas to date. Beautifully formed, the flowers stand up to wet weather very well. They are fragrant and are borne on sturdy upright stems. Vigorous bedding habit. Sponsored commercially to promote the platinum industry.

Varieties of similar colour (rich crimson-scarlet velvet) not illustrated:

Baccara

Parentage Happiness × Independence
Raiser Meilland
Year of introduction 1956
A fine cut flower variety which lasts extremely well. For a long time the principal red Rose in florists shops. Dislikes wet weather and is not suitable for garden culture.

Ena Harkness

Parentage Southport × Crimson Glory
Raiser Norman
Year of introduction 1946
Rich crimson-scarlet blooms of good shape, for years the principal red Hybrid Tea grown in Britain, but its unfortunate tendency to hang its head when fully out has lost it popularity. Best in cool weather. Named for Mrs Harkness, the wife of the introducer.

Pharoah

Parentage (Happiness × Independence) × Suspense
Raiser Meilland
Year of introduction 1967
Vivid scarlet blooms of quite unfading intensity. The dark green glossy foliage needs protection from Black Spot. No fragrance.

Red Planet

Parentage Red Devil × (Brilliant × seedling)
Raiser Dickson
Year of introduction 1969
A fine crimson Hybrid Tea now eclipsed by Precious Platinum, one of its progeny, from the same raiser.

Troika   (*illustrated*)

Parentage   Not published
Raiser   Poulsen
Year of introduction   1972
Large flowers of good shape, orange-bronze in colour. The outer petals are deeper reddish-orange. Very free flowering, the growth is upright. Smooth stems, heavy bright green foliage. Very fragrant. Quite the best of its shade.

Varieties of similar colour (orange-bronze-shaded red) not illustrated:

Mojave

Parentage   Charlotte Armstrong × Signora
Raiser   Armstrong
Year of introduction   1953
The long straight stems, with few thorns, bearing slim blooms of burnt-orange shaded copper-red make this a favourite for cutting. Unfortunately, the cropping is not sufficiently free to make this a worthy subject for the cut flower grower.

Mrs Sam McGredy

Parentage   (Donald MacDonald × Golden Emblem) × (seedling × the Queen Alexandra Rose)
Raiser   McGredy
Year of introduction   1929
A famous Rose of incomparable beauty. The copper-salmon blooms are greatly enhanced by the young reddish-bronze foliage. A hardy variety which dislikes cold, heavy soils. Repays dead-heading more than most; otherwise produces very large heps which deter the production of further flowers.

Signora   (synonym Signora Piero Puricello)

Parentage   Julien Potin × Sensation
Raiser   Aicardi
Year of introduction   1936
A blend of flame, orange-yellow and pink, very sweetly scented with a ragged edge to each petal. The juvenile shoots are prone to mildew and therefore distortion.

Serenade

Parentage   Sonata × Mev. H. A. Verschuren
Raiser   Boerner
Year of introduction   1949
Elegant blooms of copper-pink with orange shading. Bronze foliage borne on vigorous wiry growth, though somewhat thin.

Typhoo Tea   (*illustrated*)

Parentage Fragrant Cloud × Arthur Bell
Raiser McGredy
Year of introduction 1975
A tall grower well-clothed with large heavy foliage and bearing very fragrant blooms of scarlet-rose with cream reverse.

Varieties of similar colour (red and white bi-colour) not illustrated:

Oriana

Parentage Not known
Raiser Tantau
Year of introduction 1966
A brilliant scarlet and white bi-colour. The blooms are borne on a strong upright stem. Dark foliage.

Perfecta   (synonym Kordes' Perfecta)

Parentage Spek's Yellow × Karl Herbst
Raiser Kordes
Year of introduction 1957
Large well-shaped, high-centred fragrant blooms of creamy white tipped and flushed crimson. Vigorous upright growth.

Rose Gaujard

Parentage Peace × Opera seedling
Raiser Gaujard
Year of introduction 1957
Large blooms of cherry-red with silvery white reverse. Little or no fragrance. Strong upright growth, heavy, disease-resistant foliage. Has a tendency to produce split blooms, so is not wholly reliable for the exhibitor.

Stella

Parentage Horstmann's Jubiläumrose × Peace
Raiser Tantau
Year of introduction 1958
Full creamy white blooms of good shape and large size, shaded and edged carmine, deepening with age to shaded pink. Vigorous upright growth.

Isabel De Ortiz   (synonym Isabel Ortiz)

Parentage Peace × Perfecta
Raiser Kordes
Year of introduction 1962
A large shapely bloom of deep pink with silvery reverse. Fragrant, but intolerant of wet weather.

Whisky Mac   (synonym Whisky)   (*illustrated*)

Parentage   Unknown
Raiser   Tantau
Year of introduction   1961
Fragrant harvest-gold blooms of medium to small size, freely produced on a neat compact plant. The young growth, sometimes prone to mildew, is an attractive bronze-purple, maturing to deep bronze-green. Named after that excellent cold weather potion, a mixture of Scotch whisky and ginger wine.

Varieties of similar colour (golden apricot) not illustrated:

Apricot Silk

Parentage   Unknown × Souv. de Jacques Verschuren
Raiser   Gregory
Year of introduction   1965
A deep apricot bloom of medium size borne on a bush of medium growth, well-clothed with dark green-tinted-bronze foliage, which has an unfortunate susceptibility to mildew in areas where this disease is rife.

Doris Tysterman

Parentage   Peer Gynt × Seedling
Raiser   Tysterman
Year of introduction   1975
Elegant medium-sized blooms of deep gold, shaded bronze. Taller than 'Whisky Mac', which it resembles, though of brighter hue. Fragrant. Named after Doris, wife of Bill Tysterman of Wisbech, Cambridgeshire, both good friends to Rosarians the world over.

Litakor   (synonyms Lolita and Korlita)

Parentage   Not published
Raiser   Kordes
Year of introduction   1973
Perfectly shaped blooms of bright copper-gold; strong upright growth, very free flowering. A fine Rose for the flower arranger.

Sutter's Gold

Parentage   Charlotte Armstrong × Signora
Raiser   Swim
Year of introduction   1950
Yellow with orange-red veinings, the buds are deep orange shot with red, and the fully-matured flower is pale creamy yellow. Very fragrant and free-flowering. Upright habit, few thorns. Named to commemorate the finding of gold on the land of John Augustus Sutter in 1848 in California. Sutter saw his land over-run, his herds slaughtered by miners and by 1852 he was bankrupt.

Floribunda Roses

It was in the early 1950's that one became aware of the term 'Floribunda', a word coined in the United States to describe an emergence of such varieties as 'Fashion' and 'Masquerade'. To find their origins, however, we must go back to 1924 in Denmark when Svend Poulsen began to cross the polyantha pom-poms (a race of bedding Roses which has now lost favour because of its susceptibility to mildew) with the Hybrid Teas. The result was a completely new type, officially then classified as Hybrid Polyanthas, but popularly known throughout the world as the 'Poulsen' Roses. The best known were those that the Danish master named after members of his family, 'Else', 'Kirsten', 'Karen' and 'Anne'. Other well-known ones are 'Poulsen's Copper', 'Poulsen's Pink', Poulsen's Yellow', etc. In the main they were typified by their upright habit, clustered flowers and rapid repeat flowering characteristics.

In the 1930's and 1940's British breeders, notably LeGrice, McGredy, Dickson and Robinson, hastened the development of the class with many varieties, all of which achieved fame in their day and were still called Hybrid Polyanthas.

With the arrival of the 'Floribunda' from the United States, it was felt that the class had changed sufficiently for the new title to be accepted. The other term 'Grandiflora' was found unacceptable botanically.

The Royal National Rose Society, in 1971, described Floribunda Roses as bearing their flowers in large trusses or clusters in which many open at the same time, on plants which normally grow to a height suitable for bedding purposes. At the same time, the Royal National Rose Society heralded the arrival of yet another variation, the 'Floribunda-Hybrid Tea Type'. As is their way, the hybridists, seeking improvements in colour, flower-shape, and performance, had re-crossed the existing cultivars with the latest in the Hybrid Tea clan, which you will remember had already received an infusion of new blood from other species. The resultant varieties, if dis-budded to one flower on a stem, give decorative Hybrid Tea flowers, but will otherwise flower in clusters as is their normal habit.

It is obvious that this class is still evolving and it is easy to foresee that eventually the Hybrid Teas and the Floribundas will belong under one heading. It would be simple to give the new class an academically acceptable name, but with the garden-loving public in mind, an easy, attractive, yet botanically correct title must be the aim.

Floribunda roses at Cap d'Antibes. ▶

Ann Aberconway

(illustrated)

Parentage Arthur Bell × Seedling
Raiser Mattock
Year of introduction 1976
Apricot-yellow, with buff and pink shading. Blooms of good Hybrid Tea shape and size borne in clusters of medium size. Fragrant, an upright, vigorous grower with dark, leathery foliage. Ann Aberconway is the wife of Lord Aberconway, the President of the Royal Horticultural Society.

Varieties of similar colour (apricot-orange) not illustrated:

Apricot Nectar

Parentage Unnamed seedling × Spartan
Raiser Jackson and Perkins
Year of introduction 1966
Creamy apricot blooms with apricot-orange shading in the deeper recesses of the flower. Slight, but perceptible fragrance. A moderate grower of medium height.

Iced Ginger

Parentage An Anne Watkins seedling
Raiser Dickson
Year of introduction 1971
Apricot-buff Hybrid Tea shaped flowers of medium size, whose buds are tinted deep copper-red. The growth is of medium height with a very upright habit.

Vesper

Parentage Unknown
Raiser LeGrice
Year of introduction 1966
Burnt-orange blooms of medium size. The growth is vigorous and upright, the foliage dark green and tinted bronze-red.

Southampton

Parentage (Ann Elizabeth × Allgold) × Yellow Cushion
Raiser Harkness
Year of introduction 1971
Apricot-orange Hybrid Tea shaped blooms with some fragrance, are borne on tall, upright plants, well-clothed with dark green glossy foliage.

Arthur Bell   (*illustrated*)

Parentage   Clare Grammerstorf × Piccadilly
Raiser   McGredy
Year of introduction   1965
Large fragrant blooms of good Hybrid Tea shape. The bright golden yellow colour is retained until the flower is fully open and then fades to a not unpleasing creamy yellow. Strong, healthy upright growth, with few thorns. The leathery foliage is semi-glossy and dark green. Named for the famous Scotch Whisky distillery.

Varieties of similar colour (golden yellow) not illustrated:

Chinatown

Parentage   Columbine × Clare Grammerstorf
Raiser   Poulsen
Year of introduction   1963
Very double blooms of clear yellow opening to a rosette-shaped flower, having a tendency to age with a blush-pink edge in hot summers. A tall shrubby grower with luxuriant light green foliage, ideal for the back of a border.

Courvoisier

Parentage   Elizabeth of Glamis × Casanova
Raiser   McGredy
Year of introduction   1970
Fragrant Hybrid Tea shaped blooms of creamy amber-yellow, reminiscent of that famous brandy whose name it bears. The growth is moderate in height, but not robust enough to flourish in brashy soils, though excellent in rich loams.

Gold Marie

Parentage   Masquerade × Golden Main
Raiser   Kordes
Year of introduction   1958
Orange-golden buds splashed orange-red, opening to large semi-double somewhat ragged blooms of golden yellow, sometimes lightly shaded pink. Vigorous shrubby habit, of great charm and very fragrant.

Kiskadee

Parentage   Not known
Raiser   McGredy
Year of introduction   1973
Golden yellow blooms of mellow hue borne in large trusses on a healthy plant of medium, upright habit. Kiskadee is the onomatopoeic name of a Caribbean bird (or a rum marketed in Ireland).

Bonfire Night

Parentage Tiki × Variety Club
Raiser McGredy
Year of introduction 1971

The well-shaped blooms look like small Hybrid Teas and are of a pleasing deep orange. They are splashed yellow and scarlet and are borne on a bush of medium to low growth, well-clothed with dark green foliage.

Varieties of similar colour (orange and yellow) not illustrated:

Esther Ofarim

Parentage Colour Wonder × Zorina
Raiser Kordes
Year of introduction 1970

Medium-sized blooms of brightest orange-scarlet with glowing gold reverse to the petals. The low branching bush may be affected by frost in a hard winter. On the other hand, this is an excellent variety to grow in a glasshouse. Named for the Israeli singer.

Manx Queen (synonym Isle of Man)

Parentage Shepherd's Delight × Circus
Raiser Dickson
Year of introduction 1963

Deep orange flowers with carmine shading on the outer petals. Blooms borne in large trusses, with good autumn repeat. Glossy abundant disease-resistant foliage. The record of this variety is marred by a dearth of mid-summer blooms.

Shepherdess

Parentage Allgold × Peace
Raiser Mattock
Year of introduction 1967

Soft golden yellow flowers whose petals are edged carmine-pink, borne in trusses with an occasional bloom borne on its own which can reach 'box bloom' size. Large leathery dark green foliage on a bushy plant of medium size and habit.

Princess Michiko

Parentage Spartan × Circus
Raiser Dickson
Year of introduction 1966

Semi-double blooms of coppery-orange, fading to dullish russet-red. Vigorous upright growth, bearing smallish semi-glossy dark green foliage, which has an unfortunate tendency to attacks of Black Spot. Named for the Crown Princess of Japan.

Captain Cook

Parentage   Not known
Raiser   McGredy
Year of introduction   1977
The unusually bright vermilion colour of Captain Cook causes one to think that surely the ultimate in brilliance has been achieved in the plant breeder's palette, but I am certain that the future holds as many surprises to delight the Rose lover. A vigorous bushy plant of good bedding habit, bearing semi-double blooms opening flat to show a mass of golden stamens. Named, of course, after the explorer.

Varieties of similar colour (bright vermilion) not illustrated:

Anne Cocker

Parentage   Highlight × Colour Wonder
Raiser   Cocker
Year of introduction   1971
Bright vermilion very double rosette-shaped flowers having a golden shade at the base of each petal. The blooms are borne in large trusses on a rather leggy, thorny plant. Named after the wife of the raiser.

Mary Sumner

Parentage   (Orangeade × Margot Fonteyn) × [Elizabeth of Glamis × (Little Darling × Goldilocks)]
Raiser   McGredy
Year of introduction   1975
Coppery vermilion semi-double blooms borne in great profusion on an upright branching plant, whose strong glossy foliage impresses for sheer exuberant healthiness Named after the founder of the Mother's Union in its Centenary year.

Poppy Flash

Parentage   (Dany Robin × Fire King) × (Alain × *R. chinensis mutabilis*)
Raiser   Meilland
Year of introduction   1972
Large semi-double blooms of orange-vermilion set on a vigorous bush of medium height, with deep green foliage.

Orangeade

Parentage   Orange Sweetheart × Independence
Raiser   McGredy
Year of introduction   1959
Semi-double blooms opening flat to show petals of bright orange-vermilion and bright golden stamens. Vigorous bushy growth, but some susceptibility to Black Spot seems to be creeping into this variety.

Congratulations   (synonym Kordes Sylvia)   (*illustrated*)

Parentage   Not published
Raiser   Kordes
Year of introduction   1978
A tall-growing bush, somewhat reminiscent of The Queen Elizabeth Rose, well clothed with rich luxuriant foliage. The blooms are of porcelain-pink and have superb shape.

Varieties of similar colour (soft pink) not illustrated:

Dearest

Parentage   Seedling × Spartan
Raiser   Dickson
Year of introduction   1960
Double flowers of mid to light pink, the petals are somewhat soft which makes resistance to the effects of weathering poor, but the fragrance is most pronounced. The medium to short growth is rather upright and the dark green foliage glossy, but liable to both Black Spot and rust in areas where disease is prevalent.

English Miss

Parentage   Dearest × Sweet Repose
Raiser   Cant
Year of introduction   1978
Very fragrant full double blooms of silvery pink edged and shaded deep pink, borne in well-spaced trusses on a bush of vigorous bushy growth.

The Queen Elizabeth Rose

Parentage   Charlotte Armstrong × Floradora
Raiser   Lammerts
Year of introduction   1955
Clear soft mid-pink blooms of moderate fullness borne sometimes singly, and sometimes in clusters. The growth is vigorous and tall and is well-clothed with dark glossy foliage.

Vera Dalton

Parentage   Paul's Scarlet Climber × (Mary × The Queen Elizabeth Rose)
Raiser   Norman
Year of introduction   1961
A healthier Floribunda than 'Dearest', but lacking that variety's fragrance, is by no means as widely grown. Vigorous branching habit and bearing blooms of clear soft pink.

Centurion (illustrated)
Parentage Seedling × Franklin Engelmann
Raiser Mattock
Year of introduction 1975
Hybrid Tea shaped blooms of velvety crimson-scarlet borne in trusses on a vigorous bush of medium height and upright, branching habit. A variety introduced by the family firm of the writer to celebrate its centenary year. Varieties of similar colour not illustrated:

Frensham
Parentage Floribunda seedling × Crimson Glory
Raiser Norman
Year of introduction 1946
Large trusses of deep crimson-scarlet with double blooms borne freely over a long period. Vigorous, bushy growth but an unfortunate tendency to mildew crept into Frensham in the 1960's, losing a great deal of popularity for this variety.

Stephen Langdon
Parentage Karl Herbst × Sarabande
Raiser Sanday
Year of introduction 1969
Rich crimson semi-double blooms borne in trusses on a vigorous upright bush of branching habit. Deep green, healthy foliage.

Iceberg (synonyms Schneewitchen, Fée des Neiges)   (*illustrated*)
Parentage Robin Hood × Virgo
Raiser Kordes
Year of introduction 1958
A shrubby grower with pure white semi-double flowers borne in large decorative trusses. A medium tall variety, outstanding for massing or as a background to shorter-growing Roses. Varieties of similar colour (white) not illustrated:

Ice White (synonym Vison Blanc)
Parentage Mme Leon Cuny × (Orange Sweetheart × Cinnabar)
Raiser McGredy
Year of introduction 1966
Large double white blooms of Hybrid Tea form, in clusters very freely borne. The foliage is glossy and the growth of medium height.

Isis
Parentage Shepherdess × Vera Dalton
Raiser Mattock
Year of introduction 1973
Large Hybrid Tea shaped fragrant blooms of white, slightly tinted pink at the heart of opening petals. The short, sturdy growth is amply clothed in large healthy foliage. Named for the River Thames at Oxford.

Elizabeth of Glamis   (synonym Irish Beauty)   (*illustrated*)

Parentage   Spartan × Highlight
Raiser   McGredy
Year of introduction   1964
Fragrant double blooms of glowing coral-salmon. Vigorous upright, yet compact growth of medium height. Dislikes cold wet clay soils when it will be attacked by most of the more feared Rose diseases. Nevertheless, an excellent variety. Named for H.M. Queen Elizabeth, the Queen Mother.

Varieties of similar colour (light salmon-vermilion) not illustrated:

City of Leeds

Parentage   Evelyn Fison × (Spartan × Red Favourite)
Raiser   McGredy
Year of introduction   1966
Rich salmon-rose blooms of neat Hybrid Tea form, borne in great profusion throughout the season. Foliage of dark bronze-green with an upright branching plant of medium height.

Irish Mist

Parentage   Orangeade × Mischief
Raiser   McGredy
Year of introduction   1967
Large shapely blooms of light vermilion borne in well-balanced trusses on a bush of medium-low growth. Slight fragrance. Named for a commercial sponsor.

Scented Air

Parentage   A Spartan seedling × The Queen Elizabeth Rose
Raiser   Dickson
Year of introduction   1967
The full flowers of glowing soft salmon are larger than most floribundas and have a refreshing fragrance. A handsome upright grower of medium to tall height, clothed with luxuriant mid-green foliage.

The Sun

Parentage   (Little Darling × Goldilocks) × Irish Mist
Raiser   McGredy
Year of introduction   1974
Fragrant Hybrid Tea shaped blooms of good size and of soft salmon-orange colour. A sturdy upright, medium-tall grower named after its commercial sponsor, the newspaper.

Kerryman (*illustrated*)

Parentage   Paddy McGredy × (Mme Leon Cuny × Columbine)
Raiser   McGredy
Year of introduction   1970
Large Hybrid Tea shaped blooms in unusual shades of pink, the colour intensifying at the edge of the petal as the bloom ages giving the effect of an almost white centre. One of the first varieties to start flowering, on a medium-low bush.

Varieties of similar colour (soft peach and rose pink) not illustrated:

Sea Pearl

Parentage   Perfecta × Montezuma
Raiser   Dickson
Year of introduction   1964
Full blooms of Hybrid Tea shape and size, of salmon-pink and pale orange, with paler reverse, borne in well-shaped trusses. The vigorous tall plant is clothed with large medium green foliage. Despite its clusters, it makes an admirable cutting Rose.

Tip Top

Parentage   Unknown
Raiser   Tantau
Year of introduction   1963
Fragrant salmon-pink, very full blooms on a vigorous dwarf bushy plant. The matt medium green foliage needs protection from Black Spot.

Pink Parfait

Parentage   First Love × Pinocchio
Raiser   Swim
Year of introduction   1962
Elegant Hybrid Tea shaped blooms of medium to light pink slightly shaded yellow at the base of the petals. Slight fragrance. Vigorous upright branching habit. The foliage is medium green and semi-glossy and borne in abundance.

Escapade

Parentage   Pink Parfait × Baby Faurax
Raiser   Harkness
Year of introduction   1967
Semi-double flowers of magenta-rose, which open flat to show golden stamens. The colour, unusual in modern Roses, commends it to be planted with the old garden Roses to blend with, and to extend the flowering period of that section.

Korresia   (synonym Friesia)   (*illustrated*)

Parentage   Unknown
Raiser   Kordes
Year of introduction   1973
Clear bright yellow blooms of Hybrid Tea shape with a very sweet fragrance, make this possibly the best yellow Rose today. Neat, compact growth of medium height, well-clothed with glossy light green foliage.

Varieties of similar colour (bright yellow) not illustrated:

Allgold

Parentage   Goldilocks × Ellinor Le Grice
Raiser   Le Grice
Year of introduction   1956
Semi-double blooms of bright deep yellow, a bush of medium height. The glossy foliage is dark green and though on the small side, is abundant. For years the leading yellow Floribunda, a position it has now lost to Korresia.

Golden Treasure   (synonym Goldschatz)

Parentage   Not known
Raiser   Tantau
Year of introduction   1964
Brilliant golden yellow blooms of good size and shape. The foliage is deep green and leathery with an unfortunate susceptibility to Black Spot.

Moon Maiden

Parentage   Fred Streeter × Allgold
Raiser   Mattock
Year of introduction   1970
Creamy yellow fragrant flowers with a shading of deeper, almost buff hues. A bushy grower of medium height. Named on the day of the first moon walk to commemorate that historic occasion.

Sunsilk

Parentage   Pink Parfait × A Redgold seedling
Raiser   Fryer
Year of introduction   1974
Pure lemon-yellow blooms of perfect Hybrid Tea form and size. It is sometimes classified as an Hybrid Tea, but because of its parentage, it must find its place among the Floribundas. Vigorous, upright branching growth.

Masquerade

(illustrated)

Parentage Goldilocks × Holiday
Raiser Jackson and Perkins
Year of introduction 1949
Semi-double blooms of medium size in large trusses. The yellow buds, on opening, turn salmon-pink and then dark red before dropping, giving the effect of a multicoloured mass of flower. The Rose was such a sensation on its introduction that it soon became a byword.

Varieties of similar colour (yellow and red bi-colour) not illustrated:

Circus

Parentage Fandango × Pinocchio
Raiser Swim
Year of introduction 1956
A fairly vigorous yet compact grower of upright habit, its very double flowers of creamy yellow become flushed and edged pink, deepening with age. Some Black Spot.

Redgold

Parentage [(Karl Herbst × Masquerade) × Faust] × Piccadilly
Raiser Dickson
Year of introduction 1967
Golden yellow Hybrid Tea shaped blooms edged bright red, some fragrance. Vigorous upright growth with glossy foliage which needs protection from Black Spot.

Rumba

Parentage (Poulsen's Bedder × Floradora) × Masquerade
Raiser Poulsen
Year of introduction 1959
Smallish rosette-shaped blooms of golden yellow, heavily overlaid pink, changing to deep red. Some fragrance; a bushy grower of moderate vigour.

Shepherd's Delight

Parentage A Masquerade seedling × Joanna Hill
Raiser Dickson
Year of introduction 1958
A bright orange and yellow seedling from 'Masquerade' with some fragrance. Vigorous upright growth and bright dark green foliage, which may need protection from Black Spot.

Priscilla Burton   (synonym Macrat)   (*illustrated*)
Parentage (Maxi × [Evelyn Fison × (Orange Sweetheart × Frühlingsmorgen)]
Raiser McGredy
Year of introduction 1978
A brilliant silvery white and carmine-purple bi-colour. The semi-double blooms open to show a white eye and prominent golden yellow stamens. The blooms are beautifully set off by abundant dark green glossy foliage. Named for the wife of the Chairman of Fisons.

Other varieties of various shades in the hand-painted series (not illustrated):

Eye Paint
Parentage [(Little Darling × Goldilocks) × Evelyn Fison × (Coryana × Tantau's Truimph)] × Picasso
Raiser McGredy
Year of introduction 1976
A fine shrubby variety carrying huge trusses of single flowers of brightest scarlet with a white 'eye' and golden stamens. A vigorous variety, with glossy foliage, it can be grown either as a medium bedding variety or, if not pruned too hard, will make a most spectacular shrub.

Matangi
Parentage [(Little Darling × Goldilocks) × Evelyn Fison × (*R. macrophylla coryana* × Tantau's Triumph)] × Picasso
Raiser McGredy
Year of introduction 1973
An exceptional member of Sam McGredy's family of hand-painted Roses. The double flowers of bright orange-vermilion are sometimes edged silver with a reverse of silvery white, sweetly fragrant. The neat growth is well-clothed with plentiful bronze-green foliage. Matangi is the Maori word for 'breeze' and is also the name of a town in New Zealand.

Picasso
Parentage Marlena × [Evelyn Fison × (Orange Sweetheart × Frühlingsmorgen)]
Raiser McGredy
Year of introduction 1971
The first of the so-called hand-painted Roses named because each petal is basically a pale colour, marked with a deeper colour in varied and often irregular shapes, as if applied individually. Picasso's base colour is silvery white and is variously marked with carmine and crimson splashes. The growth of the plant is bushy with very many wiry shoots, bearing a mass of smallish, medium green leaves.

Old Master
Parentage [(Evelyn Fison × Tantau's Triumph × Coryana)] × Hamburger Phoenix × Danse du Feu)] × [Evelyn Fison × (Orange Sweetheart × Frühlingsmorgen)]
Raiser McGredy
Year of introduction 1974
Slightly fragrant blooms of deep carmine-purple, with silvery white eye and reverse of petal. Vigorous bushy habit, with glossy dark green foliage.

Marlena (*illustrated*)

Parentage   Gertrud Wesphal × Lili Marlene
Raiser   Kordes
Year of introduction   1964
A low-growing variety which makes an excellent bedder. The crimson-scarlet blooms are semi-double and are borne throughout the season in great profusion.

Europeana

Parentage   Ruth Leuwerik × Rosemary Rose
Raiser   de Ruiter
Year of introduction   1963
The deep crimson rosette-shaped flowers are borne in trusses. Unfortunately its attractive dark coppery-red foliage is plagued by mildew just as its parent, Rosemary Rose, that favourite among flower arrangers.

Lili Marlene

Parentage   (Our Princess × Rudolf Timm) × Ama
Raiser   Kordes
Year of introduction   1959
Double bright crimson blooms with a slight fragrance borne in great profusion in large trusses. It has good weather resistance. A vigorous bushy variety, it needs protection from mildew in years when it is rife.

Tornado   (synonym Kortor)   *(illustrated)*
Parentage   Europeana × Marlena
Raiser   Kordes
Year of introduction   1973
Bright glowing scarlet, full flowers with a slight fragrance, borne in neat trusses. A sturdy compact variety with dark foliage.

Satchmo
Parentage   Not known
Raiser   McGredy
Year of introduction   1970
Well-formed blooms of glowing scarlet, very freely borne in clusters on a bush of medium-low height, making this an ideal bedding variety. Named, of course, for the late, great jazzman, Louis Armstrong.

Happy Wanderer
Parentage   Not known
Raiser   McGredy
Year of introduction   1972
Bright crimson-scarlet blooms borne in trusses of good shape. The bushes are of neat compact habit and medium height.

101

Pernille Poulsen   *(illustrated)*

Parentage   Ma Perkins × Columbine
Raiser   Poulsen
Year of introduction   1965
Salmon-rose-pink, quite deep in colour when in bud, opening to a slightly lighter hue. The fragrant Hybrid Tea shaped flowers are borne in well-spaced trusses from quite early in the season. Vigorous bushy habit. Named after Pernille, eldest daughter of the hybridist, Niels Poulsen.

Varieties of similar colour (rose-pink) not illustrated:

Heaven Scent

Parentage   Pernille Poulsen × Isabel de Ortiz
Raiser   Poulsen
Year of introduction   1968
Very fragrant Hybrid Tea shaped blooms of deep rosy-salmon, borne in great profusion on a strong, healthy bush of medium height. Well clothed in light green foliage.

Paddy McGredy

Parentage   Spartan × Tzigane
Raiser   McGredy
Year of introduction   1962
Large Hybrid Tea shaped blooms of light glowing carmine, almost scarlet when in bud. A bush of moderate height bearing enormous trusses of bloom. Named after the sister of hybridist Sam McGredy.

Sunday Times   (synonym Shrubby Pink)

Parentage   (Little Darling × Goldilocks) × München
Raiser   McGredy
Year of introduction   1971
Deep pink full blooms with lighter reverse. The growth is dwarf and ground-hugging, the foliage dark green and semi-glossy.

Tony Jacklin

Parentage   City of Leeds × Irish Mist
Raiser   McGredy
Year of introduction   1972
Orange-salmon, full Hybrid Tea shaped blooms with slight fragrance. Vigorous bushy growth of medium height.

Shocking Blue   *(illustrated)*

Parentage   Not known
Raiser   Kordes
Year of introduction   1975
One of the best in this colour range, Shocking Blue is a most fragrant variety with Hybrid Tea shaped blooms of deep magenta-lilac borne very freely throughout the season on a vigorous, but compact bush of medium height. An excellent variety for the flower arranger as its blooms stand well when cut.

Varieties of similar colour (lavender and purple shades) not illustrated:

Lilac Charm

Parentage   Unknown
Raiser   LeGrice
Year of introduction   1961
Single blooms of pale lilac-mauve with red filaments bearing golden stamens, making this a variety of great charm, valued by the flower arranger. The growth is short, almost dwarf, and branching.

News

Parentage   Lilac Charm × Tuscany Superb
Raiser   LeGrice
Year of introduction   1968
Semi-double loose blooms of beetroot-reddish-purple. Vigorous upright habit, an unusual colour in modern Roses and one which blends well into the old Rose garden.

Ripples

Parentage   Unknown
Raiser   LeGrice
Year of introduction   1971
Soft mauve rosette-shaped flowers borne on a vigorous bushy plant. An unfortunate tendency to mildew mars an otherwise excellent variety.

Yesterday

Parentage   (Phyllis Bide × Shepherd's Delight) × Ballerina
Raiser   Harkness
Year of introduction   1974
Maroon-purple blooms of the small polyantha type which have a silvery base and pronounced golden stamens, borne in large clusters. A vigorous shrubby grower of slightly spreading growth.

Trumpeter   (synonym Mactru)   (*illustrated*)

Parentage   Satchmo × Seedling
Raiser   McGredy
Year of introduction   1978
Bright scarlet blooms of medium size, borne in large regular trusses, freely produced over the whole season. A healthy variety of short, compact habit.

Varieties of similar colour (bright scarlet) not illustrated:

City of Belfast

Parentage   Evelyn Fison × (Korona × Circus)
Raiser   McGredy
Year of introduction   1968
Velvety scarlet full-petalled blooms with a perceptible fragrance, borne in good trusses on a compact bush of medium height with glossy, medium green foliage.

Evelyn Fison   (synonym Irish Wonder)

Parentage   Moulin Rouge × Korona
Raiser   McGredy
Year of introduction   1962
Bright, unfading scarlet-red blooms of double rosette form, borne continuously in broad well-spaced trusses. A compact bush of medium height.

Kapai

Parentage   Not known
Raiser   McGredy
Year of introduction   1978
Vermilion red, almost russet-red at times, Kapai's blooms are borne in large trusses from very early in the season and are among the first varieties to flower. The bushy plant, of low stature, makes this an ideal bedding variety.

Topsi

Parentage   Fragrant Cloud × Fire Signal
Raiser   Tantau
Year of introduction   1972
Glowing scarlet semi-double blooms, borne continuously on a vigorous dwarf bush of compact habit, well-clothed with semi-glossy foliage which may need some protection from Black Spot.

Young Venturer
(illustrated)

Parentage   Arthur Bell × Cynthia Brooke
Raiser   Mattock
Year of introduction   1979

Apricot coloured blends of gold and soft orange, Hybrid Tea shaped blooms borne on an upright bush of medium height. Name by request of UNICEF to commemorate 'The Year of the Child', 1979.

Varieties of similar colour (apricot-orange-yellow) not illustrated:

Copper Pot

Parentage   A Spek's Yellow seedling
Raiser   Dickson
Year of introduction   1968

Fragrant copper-orange blooms of good Hybrid Tea shape, borne on a tall (leggy) plant, with glossy bronze-green foliage.

Golden Slippers

Parentage   Goldilocks × unnamed seedling
Raiser   Von Abrams
Year of introduction   1961

Well-shaped blooms of Indian-yellow, shaded pale orange, fragrant. Vigorous, compact, low-growing with glossy foliage. Some black spot.

Sir Lancelot

Parentage   Vera Dalton × Woburn Abbey
Raiser   Harkness
Year of introduction   1967

Bright apricot-yellow semi-double blooms make this outstanding when well grown, but the variety has increasingly shown a distressing tendency to both Black Spot and mildew.

Woburn Abbey

Parentage   Masquerade × Fashion
Raiser   Sidey and Cobley
Year of introduction   1962

Orange and yellow blooms with red shading, fragrant. A vigorous branching bush with dark green leathery foliage, which needs protection from mildew to which it is prone.

Zambra

Parentage   (Goldilocks × Fashion) × (Fashion × Goldilocks)
Raiser   Meilland
Year of introduction   1961

A brilliantly coloured Floribunda whose blooms are orange and yellow. The glossy medium green foliage may need protection from disease.

Miniature Roses

It has been said that there is botanical evidence for strains of miniature forms of *R. chinensis* as garden cultivars in China over thousands of years, but it seems certain that there has been no miniature species discovered from the wild.

The introduction of *R. roulettii* in 1920 from its discovery on a window ledge of a cottage in the Swiss Jura Mountains, where it has been known for at least 150 years, led to the miniature Rose as we know it today. Interest in this section is growing by leaps and bounds with valuable work being carried out by the world's Rose hybridists, including several who specialise in miniatures alone.

Besides crossing and re-crossing the many miniatures, other species are now being used in breeding and in the background of many new and recent introductions, the influence of *R. multiflora, R. roxburghii, R. rugosa, R. wichuriana* and the moss Roses is well documented.

The pioneers of the modern miniature Rose, Jan de Vink of Holland and Pedro Dot of Spain, have been joined by McGredy of New Zealand, Kordes of Germany, Meilland of France, and by that most prolific breeder and innovator of the Miniature Rose, Ralph Moore of the USA.

There is a perennial argument about what a Miniature Rose actually is. The Royal National Rose Society in its *Roses, A Selected List of Varieties* defines them as, 'Very dwarf re-current flowering bushes from 6–12 in (15 to 30 cm) or so in height with tiny flowers often perfectly formed.' This has been contradicted by some who insist that a miniature should grow no more than 9 in (about 25 cm) in height, and by others who recognise varieties growing up to 18 in (45 cm). Whatever the claims, any restriction would cause many worthwhile cultivars to be left out of the list.

Personal preference will dictate where and how Miniatures are grown. They make excellent pot plants for the green house, heated or unheated; as subjects for planting in patio pots they are superb; and by selection of the more vigorous bushy varieties, are excellent for planting in formal beds.

Pruning may be severe or selective according to the desired effect. A great deal depends on the type of plant being grown. Should it be on its own roots, i.e. grown from a cutting, pruning may be quite hard. If budded or grafted, severe pruning may produce one or two extra-large shoots, causing an imbalance to the general effect.

The Miniature Rose Gardens, Royal National Rose Society, St Albans. ▶

Angela Rippon (synonyms Ocaru, Ocarina)
Raiser De Ruiter
Year of introduction 1978
A bushy little grower of great charm, the 1 in (2 cm) wide flowers are of bright salmon-pink.

Bit o'Sunshine
Parentage Copper Glow × Zee
Raiser Moore
Year of introduction 1956
Semi-double (18–20 petals), fragrant, bright yellow flowers borne on 1 ft high (30 cm) plant.

Colibre
Parentage Goldilocks × Perla de Montserrat
Raiser Meilland
Year of introduction 1959
Small double blooms of bright orange-yellow with slight fragrance, borne very freely on a bushy dwarf plant. The glossy dark green foliage may be prone to Black Spot in some areas.

Coralin (synonyms Carolin, Carolyn, Karolyn)
Parentage Mephisto × Perle D'Alcanada
Raiser Dot
Year of introduction 1955
A vigorous dwarf, bronze-tinted dark green foliage and full, almost globular flowers of coral-red to deep coral-pink.

Dwarfking (synonym Zwergkönig)
Parentage World's Fair × Tom Thumb
Raiser Kordes
Year of introduction 1957
Full blooms (26 petals) of velvety crimson, fading to carmine, very good shape. The 1 ft high (30 cm) growth is vigorous and bushy and the semi-glossy foliage is abundant.

Easter Morning
Parentage Golden Glow × Zee
Raiser Moore
Year of introduction 1960
Very double ivory-white blooms of good shape, borne in great abundance on a 1 ft high (30 cm) bush of compact habit.

Frosty
Parentage (*R. wichuraiana* × seedling) × self
Raiser Moore
Year of introduction 1953
Very pale pink buds opening to clear white double flowers with honeysuckle-like fragrance. The growth is compact and spreading, rather like a miniature ground cover plant.

'Royal Salute'. ▶

Gold Pin
Parentage Unnamed seedling × Arthur Bell
Raiser Mattock
Year of introduction 1974
A vigorous bush plant with light green, glossy foliage. The semi-double blooms are of bright buttercup-yellow with little or no fading. Fragrant.

Little Sunset
Parentage Seedling × Tom Thumb
Raiser Kordes
Year of introduction 1967
Salmon-pink semi-double blooms with yellow shadings, borne in clusters. Small light green foliage.

Mon Tresor (synonyms Maid Marion, Red Imp)
Parentage Ellen Poulsen × Tom Thumb
Raiser de Vink
Year of introduction 1951
Small deep crimson flowers of under one inch (about 2 cm) across, very double (45–60 petals) with a slight fragrance.

114

▲ 'Wee Man'.

New Penny
Parentage (*R. wichuraiana* × Floradora) × unnamed seedling
Raiser Kordes
Year of introduction 1962
Orange-red buds opening to coral-pink blooms with slight fragrance. Glossy, leathery foliage.

Perle D'Alcanada (synonyms Perla de Alcanada, Baby Crimson, Pearl of Canada, Titania, Wheatcrofts Baby Crimson)
Parentage Perle des Rouges × Rouletti
Raiser Dot
Year of introduction 1944
Tiny buds of oval shape, opening to semi-double blooms of deep carmine-red. Dark glossy foliage, dainty compact bush.

Pour Toi (synonyms Pari Ti, For You, Wendy)
Parentage Eduard Toda × Pompom de Paris
Raiser Dot
Year of introduction 1946
Dainty white blooms of good shape having a yellow tint to the base of each petal. Compact, upright habit.

115

Rosina   (synonym Josephine Wheatcroft)
Parentage   Eduardo Toda × Rouletti
Raiser   Dot
Year of introduction   1951
Perfect small blooms of sunflower-yellow held on dainty clusters on upright bushes of branching habit. Very free flowering.

Rosmarin
Parentage   Tom Thumb × Decapo
Raiser   Kordes
Year of introduction   1965
Small, fragrant, globular blooms of 1 in ($2\frac{1}{2}$ cm) across, changing in colour from a light pink in cool weather, to a light red when hot, intermediate temperatures produce a fascinating blend. A bushy plant with glossy, light green foliage.

Royal Salute
Parentage   New Penny × Marlena
Raiser   McGredy
Year of introduction   1977
The Rose introduced to commemorate the Silver Jubilee of Queen Elizabeth II. A very bushy plant of about 1 ft (30 cm) high, bearing double carmine-pink blooms very freely.

116

▲ 'Little Sunset'.

Scarlet Gem (synonym Scarlet Pimpernel)
Parentage (Moulin Rouge × Fashion) × (Perla de Montserrat × Perle D'Alcanada)
Raiser Meilland
Year of introduction 1961
Orange-scarlet double (55–60 petals) blooms of good shape and slight fragrance. The foliage is dark and glossy.

Starina
Parentage (Dany Robin × Fire King) × Baby Crimson
Raiser Meilland
Year of introduction 1968
A vigorous grower of bushy habit with glossy mid-green foliage. The flowers are of scarlet with orange shading.

Wee Man
Parentage Little Flirt × Marlena
Raiser McGredy
Year of introduction 1974
Semi-double fragrant blooms of light crimson-scarlet which open flat. The dwarf bush is neat and compact and the small light green foliage is semi-glossy.

117

Climbing Roses

The Climbing Roses have changed greatly within the last few decades. In early times they were not far removed from the species climbers originating in different parts of the world. One of these species, *R. wichuraiana*, produced the small-flowered Ramblers popular in the early part of the century. Vigorous though they are, they are highly susceptible to mildew and flower only in early summer. The slender, supple shoots are renewed each year after the heavy crop of bloom, which is borne on lateral growth from the previous year's stems.

The large-flowered Hybrid Tea bushes sometimes produce climbing sports, or mutations. These bloom in the summer, again as the Ramblers, on the previous year's growth. Most modern Climbers are complex hybrids into which have been bred both hardiness and the virtue of blooming the season through.

The forerunner of the range is 'The New Dawn'. A mutation from a Rambler, 'Dr W. van Fleet', it is almost the same in appearance as its parent, but with remontant or recurrent bloom. From this variety, and from the strain of hybrids bred by Wilhelm Kordes introduced in the 1950's, named 'Kordesii', have been bred the whole range of the modern Climbers. The characteristics of recurrent flowering and hardiness, have made the Climbing Rose an extremely desirable subject for all gardens, and quite the most popular means of clothing walls, fences and pergolas.

The great diversity of Climbers and Ramblers has given rise to confusion when it comes to pruning. However, the correct treatment can be decided upon, in the main, by observation. If the plant sends up new non-flowering shoots after flowering in the summer, it is a Rambler. The previous year's growth having flowered, may be removed and the replacement new growths tied in to flower next year. No real harm will be done if one or two old shoots are left to furnish the area to be covered. If the main shoots are stiff and upright and Hybrid Tea or Floribunda-type blooms are produced on lateral growths, these lateral growths should be pruned back to within two eyes from the main stem. The main stems should not be removed or shortened unless there is a replacement to tie in.

Many of the modern repeat flowering hybrids are very slow growers and require no pruning, but merely tidying up and thinning what might otherwise become an over-crowded situation.

'New Dawn'. ▶

Bantry Bay   (*illustrated*)   Repeat flowering Climber

Parentage   The New Dawn × Korona
Raiser   McGredy
Year of introduction   1967

Soft pink semi-double blooms borne in widely-spaced trusses. A vigorous plant with semi-glossy, medium green foliage.

Varieties of similar colour (soft pink) not illustrated:

Albertine   Rambler

Parentage   *R. wichuraiana* × Mrs A. R. Waddell
Raiser   Barbier
Year of introduction   1921

Deep salmon-red buds opening to light shell pink, very fragrant blooms borne in extreme profusion in early summer. The growth is very vigorous and the foliage is most abundant, but may require some protection against mildew in years when it is prevalent.

Aloha   Repeat flowering Climber

Parentage   Mercedes Gallart × The New Dawn
Raiser   Boerner (Jackson and Perkins)
Year of introduction   1955

A hardy and most disease resistant variety whose very double fragrant blooms (55 petals) are borne in profusion on a slow-growing sturdy climber. The colour is rose-pink in various degrees, suffused with salmon shades.

Climbing Cecile Brunner   Summer flowering Climber

Parentage   A sport from the bush of the same name raised by Ducher in 1880.
Discovered by Hosp in 1894

Pale pink, beautifully formed miniature blooms, borne in very great profusion on a big (20 ft or more [7 m]) vigorous grower.

Coral Dawn   Repeat flowering Climber

Parentage   (A New Dawn seedling × unnamed seedling) × unnamed seedling
Raiser   Boerner (Jackson and Perkins)
Year of introduction   1952

Very double (30–35 petals) globular soft rose-pink blooms borne in clusters on a 10 ft ($3\frac{1}{2}$ m) high plant.

Dorothy Perkins   Rambler

Parentage   *R. wichuraiana* × Mme Gabriel Luizet
Raiser   Jackson and Perkins
Year of introduction   1901

Small rose-pink flowers in large clusters, blooming in early summer on a vigorous grower. Most susceptible to mildew.

Seagull   (*illustrated*)   Rambler

Parentage   Not known
Raiser   Pritchard
Year of introduction   1907
Single pure white blooms borne in great profusion on a vigorous grower.

Varieties of similar colour (white) not illustrated:

Alberic Barbier   Rambler

Parentage   *R. wichuraiana* × Shirley Hibberd
Raiser   Barbier
Year of introduction   1900
The yellow buds open to full white flowers shaded pale yellow at the centre at midsummer; sometimes produces a few blooms in the autumn. Very vigorous growth and glossy dark green foliage.

Climbing Iceberg   Summer flowering Climber

Parentage   A sport from the dwarf bush form
Raiser   Cants
Year of introduction   1968
The famous white Floribunda in climbing form, with moderately-full blooms (25 petals) and the vigorous 10–15 ft (3–4½ m) growth is well-clothed with glossy foliage which often needs protection from mildew.

Bobbie James   Rambler

Parentage   Not known
Raiser/Introducer   Sunningdale Nurseries
Year of introduction   1961
A very free-flowering Rambler, extremely fragrant creamy white single cupped blooms borne in trusses. Vigorous growth.

Purity   Rambler

Parentage   Unnamed seedling × Mme Caroline Testout
Raiser   Hoopes Bro and Thomas
Year of introduction   1917
Large pure white semi-double flowers with a slight fragrance. The light green foliage is borne freely.

White Cockade   Repeat flowering Climber

Parentage   The New Dawn × Circus
Raiser   Cocker
Year of introduction   1969
Large white flowers with slight ivory shade at the base of the petals. Fragrant. The growth is vigorous and the foliage dark green and glossy.

Golden Showers   (*illustrated*)   Repeat flowering Climber

Parentage   Charlotte Armstrong × Capt. Thomas
Raiser   Lammerts
Year of introduction   1957
Golden yellow buds of good shape, open to paler semi-double blooms. A very free flowering variety which has colour almost continuously throughout the whole summer and autumn. A vigorous upright branching grower, with leathery dark green foliage.

Varieties of similar colour (shades of yellow) not illustrated:

Casino   Repeat flowering Climber

Parentage   Coral Dawn × Buccaneer
Raiser   McGredy
Year of introduction   1963
Soft yellow blooms, the bud is deeper in colour. It has been described by one authority as nearest in colour to McGredy's Yellow in a climber. The growth is vigorous, to about 10 ft (about 3 m), but unfortunately the foliage is susceptible to Black Spot.

Dreaming Spires   Repeat flowering Climber

Parentage   Arthur Bell × Buccaneer
Raiser   Mattock
Year of introduction   1973
Fragrant double blooms of golden yellow, in clusters. The buds are splashed bright red. The growth is very vigorous and upright, the foliage heavy and dark green. 'Dreaming Spires' is, of course, the name for Oxford 'the city of dreaming spires' of Matthew Arnold's poem.

Elegance   Summer flowering Climber

Parentage   Glenn Dale × (Mary Wallace × Miss Lolita Armour)
Raiser   Brownell
Year of introduction   1937
Full (30–40 petals) blooms of pale lemon-yellow, slightly fragrant, a most beautiful variety. A vigorous upright grower with abundant mid-green foliage. Some bloom in late summer.

Leverkusen   Kordesii Climber

Parentage   R. *kordesii* × Golden Glow
Raiser   Kordes
Year of introduction   1955
Pale creamy-yellow rosette-shaped blooms, borne in clusters on a rambler-type plant often producing sprays of bloom again in the autumn.

Grand Hotel   (*illustrated*)   Repeat Flowering Climber

Parentage Brilliant × Heidelberg
Raiser McGredy
Year of introduction 1972
Medium sized scarlet blooms of good shape borne extremely freely. The growth is moderate, reaching about 8 ft (2 m) in height.

Varieties of similar colour (scarlet) not illustrated:

Altissimo   Repeat flowering Climber

Parentage Not known
Raiser Delbard-Chabert
Year of introduction 1967
Bright deep scarlet single blooms with crimson overtones, opening to show its bright golden yellow anthers. A vigorous sturdy grower to about 15 ft ($4\frac{1}{2}$ m). May be pruned to shape to make into a most attractive shrub.

Copenhagen   Repeat flowering Climber

Parentage Seedling × Ena Harkness
Raiser Poulsen
Year of introduction 1964
Light scarlet blooms of good Hybrid Tea shape with a good fragrance. A slow grower, which takes a year or two to produce typical Climber growth to about 10 ft (3 m).

Soldier Boy   Climber

Parentage Unnamed seedling × Guinée
Raiser Le Grice
Year of introduction 1953
Charming single blooms of bright scarlet in clusters borne in great profusion in the summer and intermittently through the autumn. A fine pillar rose.

Sweet Sultan   Repeat flowering Climber

Parentage Independence × Honour Bright
Raiser Eacott
Year of introduction 1958
Very large single blooms of crimson shaded maroon, in trusses. Very fragrant.

Paul's Scarlet Climber   Rambler

Parentage Paul's Carmine Pillar × Soleil d'Or
Raiser Paul
Year of introduction 1915
Semi-double blooms of light scarlet borne in small clusters. A vigorous grower with small matt light green foliage.

Handel   (*illustrated*)   Repeat flowering Climber

Parentage   Columbine × Heidelberg
Raiser   McGredy
Year of introduction   1965

Creamy white blooms flushed pink at the edge of the petals, with slight fragrance. Perfect shape. The growth is vigorous and the foliage is dark green, tinted bronze-green. An excellent modern variety which has many admirers.

Varieties of similar colour (pale pink shades) not illustrated:

Compassion   Repeat flowering Climber

Parentage   White Cockade × Prima Ballerina
Raiser   Harkness
Year of introduction   1973

Well-shaped blooms of pale salmon-buff, with a light pink reverse. Growth is vigorous and upright reaching 7–8 ft (2–2$\frac{1}{2}$ m).

Lady Waterlow   Repeat flowering Climber

Parentage   La France de '89 × Mme Marie Lavellé
Raiser   Nabonnand
Year of introduction   1903

Pretty blooms of pale flesh-pink edged carmine and of small to medium size. The vigorous 10 ft (3 m) growth is well-clothed with pale green matt foliage.

New Dawn   Repeat flowering Climber

Parentage   Sport of Dr W. van Fleet
Raiser   Somerset Rose Nurseries
Year of introduction   1930

Double blooms of pale flesh pink, in clusters and borne on a plant of the laxe rambler type growth, well-clothed with dark green glossy foliage.

Maigold (*illustrated*) Summer flowering Climber

Parentage Poulsen's Pink × Frühlingstag
Raiser Kordes
Year of introduction 1953

Bronze-yellow semi-double blooms borne very early in the summer. Fragrant and very free flowering. The spiny growth is well-clothed with abundant glossy bright mid- to dark green foliage. An extremely hardy variety which will also grow as a free-standing wide-spreading shrub.

Varieties of similar colour (bronze and deep yellows) not illustrated:

Lawrence Johnston (synonym Hidcote Yellow)
Summer flowering Climber

Parentage Mme Eugenie Verdier × *R. foetida* 'Persiana'
Raiser Pernet-Ducher
Year of introduction 1923

Rich lemon-yellow, semi-double blooms, opening quite flat. Fragrant. Very free flowering in early summer; the growth, which is vigorous and thorny, can reach 30 ft (9 m). The mid-green foliage has a strong resemblance to that of a briar and may be mistaken for that of a sucker.

Mermaid Bracteata (repeat) Climber

Parentage *R. bracteata* × a Tea Rose
Raiser Paul
Year of introduction 1917

A unique Rose which can be temperamental, but when well grown has a host of admirers. The large single flowers are of creamy primrose-yellow, are remarkable for their prominent amber stamens, and are borne from midsummer onwards through the autumn. The unique foliage is very glossy and borne on rather brittle shoots, which grow well in shaded northern aspects, but are not entirely hardy in the coldest winters.

Royal Gold Repeat flowering Climber

Parentage Climbing Goldilocks × Lydia
Raiser Morey
Year of introduction 1957

Deep golden yellow fragrant blooms of Hybrid Tea shape and size, borne very freely on an upright growing, vigorous plant. To obtain best results from this variety, it must be planted in a warm, sheltered position.

Yellow Banksian (synonym *R. banksia lutea*) Species Climber

Year of introduction 1824. Soft yellow, small 1 in (2 cm) blooms of rosette-shape, borne in clusters, with a delicate fragrance. As the blooms are borne in late spring on sub-lateral growth (i.e. third year growth) pruning should not be carried out. A very large grower in favourable climates such as the Mediterranean. In temperate zones it must be grown in warm sites and where the winters are hard it is best grown under glass.

Schoolgirl   (*illustrated*)   Repeat flowering Climber

Parentage   Coral Dawn × Belle Blonde
Raiser   McGredy
Year of introduction   1964
Large fragrant blooms of soft orange-apricot, borne throughout the summer. A tall, somewhat leggy, vigorous grower whose large glossy dark green foliage may need protection from Black Spot.

Varieties of similar colour (orange-apricot-buff yellow) not illustrated:

Gloire de Dijon   Repeat flowering Climber

Parentage   Thought to be a Tea Rose × Souv. de la Malmaison
Raiser   Jacotot
Year of introduction   1953
Fragrant rich buff-pink with orange-biscuit shading towards the centre of the opening flower. The bloom is profuse, in fact it is rarely without flowers through the season.

Joseph's Coat   Repeat flowering Climber

Parentage   Buccaneer × Circus
Raiser   Armstrong
Year of introduction   1964
Golden yellow blooms flushed reddish-pink at the edge of the petals, deepening to reddish-orange. A vigorous branching grower to about 8 ft ($2\frac{1}{2}$ m), will make an excellent free-standing shrub if pruned to about 4 ft (1.2 m).

Climbing Masquerade   Summer flowering Climber

Parentage   A sport of the dwarf bush variety
Raiser   Dillon
Year of introduction   1958
Included here because of its resemblance to Joseph's Coat. It is a vigorous grower but flowers little after the early summer.

William Allan Richardson   Noisette

Parentage   A Rêve d'Or sport
Raiser   Ducher
Year of introduction   1878
Included here out of pure sentiment. The writer's great grandfather listed it in his account book dated 1880, so he must have received it direct from the raiser. It is a small-flowered apricot-buff-yellow Climber which will grow to about 12 ft ($3\frac{1}{2}$ m), and repeat often through the season. May need protection in the hardest winters.

Swan Lake   (synonym Schwanensee)

Repeat flowering Climber

Parentage   Memoriam × Heidelberg
Raiser   McGredy
Year of introduction   1968

(illustrated)

Large very full (50 petals) blooms of white with a delicate shading of palest pink in the centre of the opening flower. The vigorous growth is quite compact from 7–9 ft (2.1–2.7 m), the foliage, which is mid-green and leathery, is prone to Black Spot.

Varieties of similar colour (pale cream – white) not illustrated:

Félicité et Perpétue

Rambler

Said to be a sport of *R. sempervirens*, though some authorities say it is a seedling.
Raiser   Jaques
Year of introduction   1827

Small pale cream full flowers borne in clusters on a vigorous-growing plant with almost evergreen foliage.

Mme Alfred Carriere

Noisettiana Climber

Parentage   Not known
Raiser   Schwartz
Year of introduction   1879

A medium-sized globular bloom of white with pale pink tints, freely produced on a large upright grower. The pale green shoots and foliage are produced in great abundance.

The Garland   (synonym Wood's Garland)

Rambler

Parentage   *R. moschata* × *R. multilflora*
Raiser   Wells
Year of introduction   1835

Semi-double fragrant blooms of white with faint pink and ivory-yellow shadings borne in large clusters in mid-summer. An excellent variety to grow into a small tree.

Wedding Day

Rambler

Parentage   *R. sinowilsonii* × seedling
Raiser   Stern
Year of introduction   1950

A very large grower suitable for growing into trees. The single very fragrant blooms start as pale creamy yellow buds, and open to white with a pale pink flush.

Sympathie   (*illustrated*)   Repeat flowering Climber

Parentage   Not known
Raiser   Kordes
Year of introduction   1964
Bright velvety scarlet full (40 petals) flowers, with some fragrance. A vigorous 10–15 ft
(3–4½ m) grower, with abundant glossy mid-green foliage. Very hardy.

Varieties of similar colour (bright crimson-scarlet) not illustrated:

Danse du Feu   (synonym Spectacular)   Repeat flowering Climber

Parentage   Paul's Scarlet Climber × *R. multiflora* seedling
Raiser   Mallerin
Year of introduction   1954
Orange-scarlet blooms with deeper shadings on the outside of its petals. Repeat flowering
habit may not establish itself until the plant is mature.

Dortmund   Kordessii Climber

Parentage   Seedling × *R. kordesii*
Raiser   Kordes
Year of introduction   1955
Repeat flowering, single blooms of crimson-scarlet with a white eye, flowering in clusters. A
vigorous branching grower with glossy dark green foliage.

Hamburger Phoenix   Kordesii Climber

Parentage   *R. kordesii* × seedling
Raiser   Kordes
Year of introduction   1955
Semi-double blooms of bright crimson borne in clusters. If not dead-headed, it will produce a
fine crop of bright red heps in autumn. The foliage is dark green and glossy.

Parkdirektor Riggers   Kordesii Climber

Parentage   *R. kordesii* × Our Princess
Raiser   Kordes
Year of introduction   1957
Semi-double blooms opening flat. Bright crimson-scarlet flowers carried in large trusses on a
vigorous upright grower to 15 ft (4½ m). May need protection from mildew.

Shrub Roses

It seems almost ridiculous to write a book on Roses and to allocate such a short section to Shrub Roses. The number of types and their historical life covers an enormous range which would justify at least ninety percent of a comprehensive treatise on the genus. However, I shall try to give some idea of their charm and, at the same time of their importance in the garden.

Before the advent of the bedding Roses, almost all cultivars, with the exception of the Climbers and Ramblers, made shrubby plants, often from 3°8 ft (1°2½ m) and more in height, and often as far across.

The most ancient and famous among the old garden Roses are the Gallicas (Rose of Provence). They figure in the lists of known forebears or ancestors of most other old Roses. It has been suggested that their fragrance is a characteristic reproduced in their descendents, among which may be counted the Damask Rose. The crimsons, reds and deep pinks of our modern Roses are probably a legacy from a *R. gallica* ancestor.

Another beauty from ancient history is the hundred-leafed (petalled) Rose or *R. centifolia*, which in its turn is thought to have resulted from a cross between *R. moschata* and *R. alba*. Confusion may occur with *R. gallica* because of its popular name 'The Rose of Provence'. Its other popular name, 'Cabbage Rose', can also cause some confusion to those who think of the Hybrid Perpetuals of the last century in that context.

We must look to the beginning of this century before the appearance of any new Shrub Roses to be introduced since the arrival of the Hybrid Perpetuals, the Teas and the Hybrid Teas. Taking Peter Lambert's seedling 'Trier', the Rev. Pemberton bred an exciting new range, which we know as the Hybrid Musks.

In recent years many hybridists have turned to other species of the genus *Rosa* in their search for new characteristics and from these resulting seedlings come some exciting additions to the Shrub Rose section.

Very little pruning is required by Shrub Roses. The removal of twiggy growth, the shortening of last summer's growth by about half, and general shaping of the plant is really all that is required. With many of the older varieties, mildew can be quite a problem, but the use of a reliable systemic Rose fungicide should keep this and any threat of Black Spot at bay.

'Schlachglut'. ▶

R. alba

From his 'Notes on the origin and Evolution of our Garden Roses', the late Dr C. C. Hurst tells us that ' × R. alba has been reported as growing wild in the Crimea and it may be that it originated there as a natural hybrid'.

The travels of R. alba and the number of times it was mentioned by early writers (Pliny described it as being cultivated by the Romans) can be taken as a classic example of the age and spread of the cultivation of the Rose.

The dominant characteristics of R. alba are the distinctive bluish-grey foliage, so noticeable that it has been compared to the bloom of the grape, fragrance, resistance to most of the pests of the Rose, and a vigorous upright habit, which seems to thrive in many of the most difficult situations. Among the varieties at present grown are:

Celestial   (also known as Céleste)

Mentiond by Miss Gertude Jekyll as 'A rose of wonderful beauty when the bud is half opened', Celestial has a host of admirers, and quite rightly so. The quality of colour is superb – a pure soft pink of great delicacy with just a hint of deeper colour within the unfolding petals. The foliage of soft greyish-green greatly enhances the full double blooms of this perfect Rose. Some years ago the Mattock collection was enriched by a particularly fine selection of Celestial collected from a garden in Orkney.

Great Maiden's Blush

One of the oldest favourites found in many cottage gardens. Because of this, the selection of various forms has led to a great number of garden cultivars, many bearing exotic names among which 'La Cuisse de Nymphe Émue', (translated as 'the thigh of the passionate nymph') has survived, probably on the strength of its name. It is an extremely vigorous grower reaching 6 ft (1.8 m) and more and is well-clothed with the typical *alba* foliage.

A slightly smaller grower credited to Kew Gardens in 1797 is Small Maiden's Blush. The blooms are large and have globular buds opening to a full flat rosette shape of creamy pink with deeper shading in the centre.

Koenigen van Danemark   (Queen of Denmark)   (*illustrated*)

Variously dated at 1809 and 1826, the raiser's name is given as Booth, but otherwise no other details are given of 'The Queen's' origin. It is a vigorous grower of 5–6 ft (1.5–1.8 m) in height and the deep pink, beautifully quartered flowers have a button centre. The dark blue-green foliage betrays an influence of some other parent on this otherwise perfect alba.

Maxima

The popularity of this *alba* through the ages has earned it many names – 'The Jacobite Rose', 'White Rose of York', 'Great Double White', 'Cheshire Rose', R. alba flore-plena. The large 3–4 in (7½–10 cm) in diameter blooms are double and flat and are borne in great profusion on a tall 8 ft (2½ m) shrub. This is the white Rose which appears in so many of the medieval flower paintings.

R. bourboniana

It will be appreciated from the folklore of the Rose that legends arise readily when one delves into historical research. It is certain that the family arrived from the Ile de Bourbon (renamed Ile de la Reunion) in France in 1819 and in England in 1822. It originated in a cross between *R. chinensis* and *R. damascena*. From the Bourbon Roses were bred the Hybrid Perpetuals and thence the Rose as we know it today. The main characteristics were a good foliage, a compact growth and most important of all remontant (repeat) blooming.

Boule de Neige

Raised by Francois Lacharme 1967. Very fragrant pure white camellia-shaped blooms opening with reflexed petals until the outer petals curve backwards towards the stem, presenting the appearance of a perfect sphere borne on a straight, stiff stem. The bush is upright, of medium height, bearing glossy dark green foliage.

Honorine de Brabant

Cupped and quartered blooms of medium size, the colour is pale pink with dainty spots and stripes of a deeper tone of lilac pink. The fragrance is rich and fruity and the abundant summer flush of bloom is followed by later blooms of better quality of colour. The shrub is extremely vigorous, growing up to about 8 ft ($2\frac{1}{2}$ m) and the green wood has few thorns and is well clothed with large mid-green foliage.

La Reine Victoria and Mme Pierre Oger

'La Reine Victoria' raised by Schwaz in 1872 produced a paler mutation (sport) introduced in 1878 by Oger and named 'Mme Pierre Oger' and which has almost eclipsed her parent. Both are identical in growth, tending to be rather upright to about 5–6 ft (1.5–1.8 m in height and are well clothed with dull green foliage which is, unfortunately, susceptible to Black Spot. The flowers of 'La Reine Victoria' are of soft rose pink, while its offspring's petals are of creamy white, delicately shading to soft pink with age. The flowers of both are globular in shape, each petal having a shell-like beauty, charming every lover of old garden Roses.

Mme Isaac Pereire

Raised by Garcon in 1881. One of the most fragrant of all Roses, with large deep rose-pink blooms, with madder-red shadings. When grown as a shrub it makes a fine upright grower to about 5–6 ft (1.5–1.8 m) but it can be grown as a pillar or as a wall climber. Early season blooms can often be mis-shaped but the later blooms are of good formation.

Souvenir de la Malmaison

Another Bourbon which can be grown as a pillar or climber to about 10 ft (3 m). Well-clothed with large leaves, the long shoots may be pruned quite short each year to encourage the strong lateral growths which will then make a neat shrub of manageable proportion. The colour is soft creamy pink and the flowers are produced in two distinct seasons, the later crop of blooms are of superb quality and colour.

Variegata di Bologna   (*illustrated*)

Large globular blooms of white with exciting stripes of deep crimson-purple, deeply fragrant, borne freely along the long arching stems. An unfortunate tendency to Black Spot mars an otherwise excellent variety.

Briar Hybrids

In this section are included a motley collection, most of them first crosses from species and are summer flowering. Included here are the fine Spinossisima hybrids raised by Wilhelm Kordes and the Penzance Hybrid sweetbriars. (*Illustrated: 'Cerise Bouquet'*)

Frühlingsgold
Parentage A spinossisima hybrid
Raiser Kordes
Year of introduction 1937
A superb shrub which can reach 8 ft (2½ m) in height. When in full flower in late May and June, it is most spectacular. The large single lemon yellow blooms are often 6 in (15 cm) and more across and have a distinctive fragrance.

Frühlingsmorgen
Parentage A spinossisima seedling
Raiser Kordes
Year of introduction 1941
One of the most beautiful of the 'Frühlings' series. Others in the series are 'Frühlingsanfang', 'Frühlingsduft', 'Frühlingschnee', 'Frühlingstag' and 'Frühlingszauber'. The petals are shaded from clear rose-pink on the outer edges to a centre of pale yellow, the whole delightfully set off by maroon stamens. There is an added bonus of a scattering of blooms in September.

Golden Chersonese
A seedling of *R. ecae* and *R. zanthina* variety 'Canary Bird'. A sweetly fragrant spring flowering hybrid species raised by Mr E. F. Allen and it combines the virtues of both parents. The deep buttercup-gold flowers smother the bush in late May, early June.

Lady Penzance
One of the Penzance hybrid sweetbriars whose sweet apple-fragrant foliage is inherited from its *R. rubiginosa* parent. Unfortunately from its pollen parent *R. foetida* it inherits the susceptibility to Black Spot. However, the flowers are unique in colour among the Briar hybrids being a delightful coppery-yellow carrying the fragrance of the sweetbriar.

Lord Penzance
Another of the *R. rubiginosa* (sweetbriar) hybrids, the other parent being Harison's Yellow (*R. harisonii*). The blooms are single and of an unusual fawn-yellow colour.

The Scotch Roses
R. spinossisima, the Scotch or Burnet Rose, a spiny or bristly briar (the literal translation of its Latin Name) is a widely suckering invasive grower, normally making a 3 ft (.9 m) thicket when grown in the garden, but merely half that height when found in its native climes. The foliage is distinctively small and fernlike and the flowers are followed by bright blackish maroon heps. At one time in the nineteenth century Scottish nurserymen were listing more than 200 different variations, but now only a few are catalogued.

144

Centifolias and Moss Roses

'The hundred-leafed Rose' of ancient times and referred to by both Theophratus and Pliny probably died out and the *centifolia* of our gardens almost certainly originated during the seventeenth century. As with many other old Roses a host of names accompanies this group such as the 'Old Cabbage Rose', the 'Provence Rose' and 'Rose des Peintres'. The large quartered blooms often have a button centre and are borne in heavy sprays on somewhat lax lateral growths of sturdy wide-spreading shrubs which often reach 5 ft (1½ m) high and 5 ft (1½ m) wide.

The Moss Rose

R. centifolia muscosa, the Moss Rose is said to have been known in southern France at the beginning of the eighteenth century and was distributed throughout France, Italy and Holland within a few years. There is little difference between the two forms of *centifolia,* however, the Moss Rose is distinguished by encrustations of moss-like glands on the sepals, calyx and flower stem. These glands exude a balsam-like (or resinous) fragrance which adds greatly to the attraction.

Centifolia Cristata (Crested Moss or Chapeau de Napoleon)   (*illustrated*)

Included here because it is not a true moss, in fact it is really quite on its own. The mossing is limited to the margins of the calyx, indeed it would seem to be merely, as Bunyard puts it, 'an exaggerated development of the sepal margins'. However this formation is so unusually like the three cornered hat worn by the Emperor Napoleon I that it warrants its popular name especially since the time of its discovery (1820) in Switzerland. The globular flower of pale rose-pink is sweetly fragrant.

Fantin La Tour

Discovered in a garden by Graham Stuart Thomas, the eminent horticulturist whose writings have made his name synonymous with the enthusiastic following for the old garden Roses. He was unable to trace the name in his researches but it was so aptly named for the great French artist that this is the name by which it is now universally known. The cupped pale pink blooms are tinted with a richer shade in the centre of the opening flower.

Provence

The best form which is often called the Cabbage Rose. However, if you are looking for a Victorian Cabbage Rose, the sort you can imagine embellishing the large picture hats of that era, do not look here, but at the Hybrid Perpetuals which follow on later pages. It has also been called 'Red Provence' to distinguish it from 'White Provence' (or 'Blanchefleur'), but this only serves to show how much the colours in the genus have been developed over the centuries. The colour is in fact deep clear pink and the flower has that deep fragrance we have come to look for in all old garden Roses.

Rose de Meaux

R. centifolia pomponia, has a dainty little pom-pom flower of soft pink and is a charmer for the posy maker. A neat grower of about 3 ft (.9 m) in height, clothed by tiny leaves which are in perfect proportion to the size of the flower.

Moss Rose varieties

Common Moss

R. centifolia muscosa, is also known as Pink Moss, Communis, and Pink Miller's Moss. The first Moss Rose, a sport from *R. centifolia* which came to Britain in 1727 from the Botanic Garden in Leyden, Holland. A mirror of the Provence Rose, but the addition of the mossing on its sepals and flower stem make the picture beloved of the Victorian posy maker and the epitome of the Valentine love token of that period.

Crested Moss   (see *R. centifolia cristata* in the previous section)

Nuits de Young

A fine variety, for many reasons. The colour is a deep velvety reddish purple encased when in bud by dark bronze-green mossing which is possibly the most aromatic of all. The flowers are quite small but are in perfect proportion to the neat foliage which amply clothes the upright growth.

Striped Moss   (Oeillet Panachee)

A small grower to about 3 ft (.9 m) in height, the little flowers are not heavily mossed, but the petals are unusually quilled and are of pale pink, flecked and striped with brightest crimson like sugar candy.

White Moss   (Centifolia muscosa alba)

Both the botanically correct titles seem rather dull besides its other names, 'White Bath' and 'Shailers White Moss'. The best of its colour, the dark green foliage and bronze-green mossing are perfect foils to the fat white buds of this old favourite. A bush of 5–6 ft (1.5–1.8 m) and more in height.

William Lobb   (synonym Duchesse d'Istrie)   (*illustrated*)

Sometimes called 'Old Velvet' and easily mistaken for 'Laneii' but that great rosarian Jack Harkness believes them to be different. 'William Lobb' is to be preferred if only to keep alive the name of a great Victorian plant collector. The newly opened blooms of maroon-purple soon fade to an attractive lavender-mauve with white shading at the centre of the flower. The shrub is inclined to be rather tall (about 8 ft [$2\frac{1}{2}$ m] in height.) Shortening the vigorous young growths produces an excellent crop of flowers and keeps the shape of the plant manageable. If unpruned and the growths are supported in the manner of a climber, a useful pillar effect is achieved.

China Roses

It is undoubted that the characteristic of continuous flowering which we now expect all modern Roses to carry is inherited from the dwarf China Rose that has been grown in the gardens of China for more than a thousand years. We are told (by Dr C. C. Hurst) that in a painting dated about 1529, a Florentine artist shows a cupid with his hands full of pink China Roses. However, it would appear that several records have dated plants 1769, 1781 and 1809, but this is really only of academic interest. The cultivar mentioned seems to have been:

Old Blush China

This is also known as 'Parson's Pink China', 'Common Monthly', 'Old Pink Daily', and 'Old Pink Monthly'. It is so easy to recognise this Rose as an ancestor of our modern Roses when one compares some of the early Hybrid Teas and some of the early Hybrid Polyanthas. It is said to be one of the parents of the Bourbon Roses 'and thus an ancestor of the Teas, Hybrid Perpetuals and Hybrid Teas'. (Dr Hurst). The semi-double soft rose-pink blooms are freely produced in clusters on a bushy plant usually growing to about 4 ft (1.2 m) high, but can be up to 10 ft (3 m).

Cecile Brunner   (Sweetheart Rose or Mignon)

Sometimes classified as a polyantha. The blooms are perfect miniatures of what we have come to call the Hybrid Tea shape and are a delightful flesh-pink. The bush is now large, but the blooms remain quite small. Sometimes a more vigorous plant is offered by nurserymen and this would appear to be 'Bloomfield Abundance', though the flowers of this variety are not as dainty. There is also a fine, vigorous climbing form.

Perle d'Or

Used to be called the yellow 'Cecile Brunner', but it would not be recognised as yellow now that we have seen modern versions of the colour. In fact, the colour can be classified as Indian yellow which could be called buff.

R. chinensis mutabilis   (*illustrated*)

No historical record seems to exist of this cultivar's introduction but it now seems to be accepted that it is the same as 'Tipo Ideale' figured by Redouté in the early part of the last century. The dainty growth is most vigorous (no, not a contradiction in terms): the daintiness is in the elegance of the shoots and the arrangement of the reddish foliage. Unfortunately it is prone to frost damage so may well be a subject for growing in a glasshouse in colder climates. If grown in a warm situation, it could reach 10 ft (3 m) in height, but this is usually attained only if grown in a sheltered position as a wall shrub. The flowers are single and are borne over a long summer season well into the autumn. The buds are of vivid orange, but with flame shadings; they change on opening through soft buff and orange-yellow to copper. Maturity even brings a coppery-pink and a slight purplish shade. Little wonder that it is compared to the modern Floribunda 'Masquerade' though one hastens to say it is not so garish.

Damask Roses

John Gerard mentioned Damask Roses in his famous herbal in 1597; before that they were reported in the Middle East by the crusaders, but for all the romanticism with which they are associated, very little seems to be actually identifiable. In fact, as Jack Harkness has it, 'Damasks are strangely elusive'. They are a rather vague family closely allied to the Gallicas, although those varieties which are classified as such are usually more vigorous but not so stiffly upright and could be described as open, lax bushes.

Gloire de Guilan

A Rose collected in the Caspian province of Iran, formerly Persia, by the late Miss Nancy Lindsay of Sutton Courtenay, a village close to the home of the author. An open sprawling shrub up to 3 ft (.9 m) with cupped and quartered blooms of clear pink.

Kazanlik

A Rose added to the Mattock collection by Miss Nancy Lindsay and reputed to be the variety most cultivated in Bulgaria for the production of Attar of Roses, a distillate of Rose perfume from the petals. A large vigorous bush whose deep pink blooms are heavily quartered with quilled petals.

Mme Hardy   (*illustrated*)

Raised in the Luxembourg Gardens in Paris, the recipient of the Empress Josephine's famous collection of Roses at Malmaison after the French Revolution. Monsieur Hardy was the director of the gardens. How nice to be remembered with the name of one of the most exciting Roses of the era, than to go down in history as Monsieur Hardy's wife! The pure white blooms have won it superlatives from every lover of old shrub Roses. Each flower is centred with a small white button. Mundane words cannot really describe the most beautiful Rose in the garden.

York and Lancaster

R. damascena versicolor is so named because it is thought that this was possibly the Rose from which the two factions plucked their emblems before the Wars of the Roses and as Graham Thomas puts it, 'which factions apparently later adopted *Rosa alba maxima* and *Rosa gallica officinalis* as their emblems'. The interest in this Rose is surely only in its historical connections. When compared with almost any other Rose, it seems rather insipid. Some flowers are pale pink, others white, and some are partly white and pink. It is unfortunately confused by some with 'Rosa Mundi', a much more worth-while Rose.

Gallicas

The history of the Gallicas is very much akin to the whole story of the genus Rosa. Its origins are lost in the mists of time and as the main ancestor of our modern Rose, it would take many pages to even summarize the theories and suppositions of botanical historians. Suffice it to say that it is found growing naturally throughout Western Asia, Europe and now even 'through many parts of North America where its introduction and distribution is credited to the earliest settlers'. (Roy E. Shepherd)

Cardinal Richelieu   Summer flowering only

A famous variety from 1840 which makes a compact bush of some 4 ft (1.2 m). A globular flower of dusky purple, fading to a purple-slate.

Charles de Mills

A compact, upright bush, until the crop of heavy open flowers causes it to bow down to the ground when it appears untidy, but for a good reason. The full petalled quartered and whorled blooms present an exotic face to the world in shades of maroon and rich dark purplish-red.

Rosa Mundi   (*illustrated*)

R. gallica versicolor is a sport from *R. gallica officinalis*, this is possibly the most popular of all the old garden Roses, first recorded in the sixteenth century. It has been connected with Fair Rosamund (Clifford), mistress of King Henry II, a story most attractive to the author as she is so closely connected with his native Oxfordshire. Alas, it must be said that the whole tale is a bit of unsubstantiated folklore. The lady in question died in 1177, whereas the Rose did not appear widely until the early seventeenth century! The colour of 'Rosa Mundi' may be described as white with extravagant red stripes and flecks, or even as the opposite way around. Whichever way one has it, the total effect is quite electric, yet still fitting into its niche of ancient Roses. It opens quite flat as though a single flower showing its golden stamens. Those who look for a more double Rose in this style may consider Camaieux.

Tuscany

Thought to be the 'Velvet Rose' of Gerards Herbal of 1597, an apt name for the intense purple-maroon blooms, whose colour is intensified by the bright golden stamens of the open bloom. Tuscany Superb, a distinct variety, has more petals and the stamens are not so prominent. Usually growing to about 3–4 ft (.9–1.2 m) and is therefore an excellent plant to grow in front of some of the larger specimens among the shrub Roses.

Hybrid Perpetuals

Originating in the early part of the nineteenth century in France from crosses between Hybrid Chinas and Portland and Bourbon Roses, they soon became the favourite Rose in the Victorian Rose garden. The Hybrid Perpetuals were easy plants to grow, usually too tall to be bedding Roses as we know them and because of this our Victorian forebears developed the technique known as 'pegging down', that is by taking new tall shoots (which often grew to 5–6 ft [1.5–1.8 m]in height), and bending them over to tie the tips of the growth down to ground level. This forced lateral growths to break from all the way up the shoot. From this developed a more sophisticated practice of stretching wires between pegs on the ground and tying the shoots at regular intervals producing a uniform effect.

Baron Girod de l'Ain   (Reverchon 1897)
A dark red, outstanding variety, with medium-sized blooms, edged with white.

Empereur du Maroc   (Guinoisseau 1858)
A short, 3 ft (.9 m) variety with smallish, very double blooms opening to a flat rosette shape of crimson-maroon. Very fragrant.

Ferdinand Pichard   (Tanne 1921)   (*illustrated*)
A modern Hybrid Perpetual making an open arching shrub of 4–5 ft (1.2–1.5 m). The spectacular flowers are of soft pink heavily streaked and splashed with crimson.

Paul Neyron   (Levet 1869)
The fat deep rose-pink buds open to enormous paeony-shaped flowers on sturdy stems. The 4 ft (1.2 m) shrub is well-clothed with heavy, light green foliage. An extremely fragrant variety.

Reine des Violettes   (Millet-Malet 1860)
An upright shrub of 3–4 ft (.9–1.2 m), it can be somewhat temperamental but worth growing for its violet to lilac-purple blooms of good shape. Very fragrant.

Roger Lambelin   (Schwartz 1890)
An unusual item of Victoriana. The small deep crimson blooms are tipped and striped with white streaks.

Souvenir du Dr Jamain   (Lacharnee 1865)
A most beautiful shade of rich damson-purple fading to the colour of a fine ruby port wine. The colour is preserved by siting it to face away from the sun (say on a west wall). An excellent pillar Rose which repeats well in early autumn when the colour can be at its finest. Very fragrant.

Vick's Caprice   (Vick 1891)
Large cup-shaped very double blooms of lilac-rose, striped and marbled white and carmine. Grows to some 3 ft (.9 m) in height, well-clothed with heavy light green foliage.

Rugosa Hybrids

From Japan and other Northern Asia countries came the 'Rugosa' or 'Ramanas Rose' 'probably from the Japanese *ramman* – blooming profusely – Webster's International Dictionary). And from that species has come the magnificent group of hybrids which has been used to remarkable effect by landscapers in mass plantings, for ground cover, as hedges, and as individual specimen shrubs. The single forms bear large heps which continue their colourful display into the autumn; the double varieties rarely produce heps.

Blanc Double de Coubert   (Cochet-Cochet 1892)
One of the most fragrant Roses of all times, and for this reason is probably one of the most widely planted rugosas in the public sector because of the tall rather leggy growth, although the foliage is of typical rugosa appearance.

Frau Dagmar Hastrup   (Frau Dagmar Hartopp)   (*illustrated*)
A very widely planted variety, as the neat compact 3–4 ft (.9–1.2 m) growth, the healthy rugosa foliage are particularly well suited to all types of planting. The single flowers are of a soft silvery-pink and are followed by handsome deep red heps.

F. J. Grootendorst   (De Goey, 1918)
Noteworthy for the picotee edges of the petals of the small flowers which are borne in clusters. The sport 'Pink Grootendorst' is better value for the garden, although neither make the superior plant which one expects, and gets, from most of the members of the rugosa family.

Hunter   (Mattock 1961)
A fine shrub, one of the first successes of the author's brother, Robert, hybridiser to the family firm. Using the modern Rose 'Independence' as the pollen parent, he has produced a vigorous shrub which produces bright crimson-scarlet double blooms, borne along the full length of the arching stems. Little or no fragrance. Hunter will grow to 6 ft high (1.8 m) and 6 ft wide (1.8 m).

Max Graf   (Bowditch 1919)
Quite different to any other rugosa hybrid, the wichuraiana (rambler) strain from its other parent has produced an exciting true ground cover Rose. Growing to 2–3 ft (.6 to .9 m) in height and 8 ft (2.5 m) and more across, with dense glossy foliage and single bright pink non-recurrent bloom, 'Max Graf' has been much used by landscape gardeners to cover steep banks.

Roseraie de l'Hay   (Cochet-Cochet 1901)
Named for one of the most famous of all Rose gardens in France, this variety is deservedly one of the most popular of all Shrub Roses. The large, very fragrant double blooms of rich crimson-purple are borne continuously through the whole summer and autumn on a dense bush of some 5–6 ft (1.5–1.8 m) in height. A variety named 'Hansa' is grown in cold, exposed northern climes, where 'Roseraie' is not hardy, but it is not so exciting.

158

Hybrid Musks

Once again the classification and naming of a group by popular consent clashes with actuality. Shepherd places them fairly and squarely with the Noisettes; Harkness with the Floribundas; The Royal National Rose Society, in line with the classification recommended by the World Federation of Rose Societies, puts them with the recurrent flowering Shrub Roses. However, to the general public, they will be known as the Hybrid Musks, as they have been since the Rev. Joseph H. Pemberton originated them.

Buff Beauty   (Pemberton 1922)

Apricot-yellow, heavily shaded buff, double rosette-shaped flowers in clusters borne on a spreading bush of medium height. Rich, fruity fragrance. Reddish foliage when young, becoming bronze-green as it matures. Some protection from mildew needed in late summer.

Cornelia   (Pemberton 1925)

The tiny buds of Cornelia are of deep salmon with apricot shading, but the flowers of $1\frac{1}{2}$ in (4 cm) open to soft rose with just a hint of their previous salmon shading. The decorative sprays of bloom, full of fragrance, are borne through the whole summer on a wide-spreading. but low shrub.

Felicia   (Pemberton 1928)   (*illustrated*)

One of the best varieties raised by Pemberton. As a young plant it may seem an insignificant pink, but in the Mattock garden it reaches 5–6 ft (1.5–1.8 m) and is full of flower from early summer to early autumn. As one might expect with 'Ophelia' given as a parent the flowers are of quite exceptional fragrance. She also carries the same hint of creamy yellow at the base of the petals.

Moonlight   (Pemberton 1913)

The dark shiny leaves, reddish-bronze when young, as are the stems, make a perfect setting to the simple creamy-white, very fragrant clusters of flowers.

Penelope   (Pemberton 1919)

Sometimes described as salmon pink, the colour of the open flowers is so pale as to appear white, though the small buds are quite deep in colour. Penelope is a very popular subject grown as a hedge, though one must wait a long time for the second flowering in the autumn.

Trier   (Lambert 1904)

Sometimes called a climber, but I would call it a shrub. Interesting because it was from this Rose that Pemberton raised his so-called Hybrid Musks. It is descended from the Noisette 'Rêve d'Or'. The blooms of creamy white have a hint of pink about them.

Modern Shrub Roses

It is not possible to put each of the cultivars listed hereunder into its correct family as I have done in the preceding pages with the Old Garden Roses. At any rate, it is probably more in line with modern thinking in the Rose world to list them so:

Angelina   (*illustrated*)   Repeat flowering

Parentage   (Super Star × Carina) × (Cläre Grammerstorf × Frühlingsmorgen)
Raiser   Cocker
Year of introduction   1975
A beautiful small shrub of about 3 ft (.9 m). The daintily shaded pink flowers open to show prominent stamens.

Ballerina   Repeat flowering

Parentage   Unknown
Raiser   Bentall
Year of introduction   1937
Apple blossom pink single flowers with white 'eye' borne in immense clusters on a compact 4 ft (1.2 m) shrub.

Cerise Bouquet   Summer flowering

Parentage   *R. multibracteata* × Crimson Glory
Raiser   Kordes
Year of introduction   1958
A big open arching and spreading shrub with an abundance of small matt grey-green foliage. The semi-double, flat blooms are of bright cherry red. Fragrant.

Constance Spry   Summer flowering

Parentage   Belle Isis × Dainty Maid
Raiser   Austin
Year of introduction   1961
A vigorous, somewhat leggy shrub which is best grown with support of a pillar, or of other shrubs when it can spread itself naturally. The large full, fragrant, soft rose-pink blooms are borne in great abundance.

Fountain   Repeat flowering

Parentage   Unknown
Raiser   Tantau
Year of introduction   1970
A Floribunda-like shrub with double well-shaped blooms of rich velvety crimson-scarlet. The shrub is vigorous and upright and well-clothed with dark green foliage which is red when in young growth.

Frank Naylor
Repeat flowering

Parentage Orange Sensation × Allgold
Raiser Harkness
Year of introduction 1978

A magnificent shrub Rose of vigorous 5–6 ft (1.5–1.8 m) spreading habit. The single blooms of deep crimson-maroon have an attractive golden zone round the stamens and are borne in large clusters.

Fred Loads
Repeat flowering

Parentage Orange Sensation × Dorothy Wheatcroft
Raiser Holmes
Year of introduction 1967

Fragrant semi-double blooms opening flat to show stamens. The vermilion-orange of this variety makes a vivid splash in the Rose garden and as a tall, upright variety, does well planted at the back of a Rose border.

Fritz Nobis
Summer flowering

Parentage Johanna Hill × Magnifica
Raiser Kordes
Year of introduction 1940

A beauty for the Rose garden in high summer, flower is cool fresh salmon-pink. A vigorous bushy grower up to 6 ft (1.8 m).

Golden Wings   Repeat flowering
Parentage   Soeur Therese × (*R. spinosissima altaica* × Ormiston Roy)
Raiser   Shepherd
Year of introduction   1956
Clear pale lemon-yellow blooms with prominent amber stamens, slight fragrance. One of the most beautiful of all modern shrub Roses, the pale green matt foliage is borne in great abundance.

Kassel   Repeat flowering
Parentage   Hamburg × Scarlet Else
Raiser   Kordes
Year of introduction   1958
A vigorous upright 6 ft (1.8 m) shrub with dusky orange-scarlet blooms of good shape held in large well-formed clusters. The semi-glossy medium green foliage is borne in great abundance and is resistant to disease and pests.

Lady Sonia   Repeat flowering
Parentage   Grandmaster × Doreen
Raiser   Mattock
Year of introduction   1960
A vigorous upright grower with glossy dark green foliage. The semi-double blooms are of deep golden yellow and have a slight fragrance.

Lavender Lassie   Repeat flowering

Raiser   Kordes
Year of introduction   1959
A low-growing (3 to 4 ft [.9 to 1.2 m]) shrub with semi-glossy light green foliage. The fragrant full rosette-shaped blooms are of lavender-pink.

Magenta   (synonym Kordes Magenta)   Repeat flowering

Parentage   A Floribunda × Lavender Pinocchio
Raiser   Kordes
Year of introduction   1955
The deep magenta-rose buds open to soft purple blooms with magenta shading. Very full and very fragrant. The clusters of bloom tend to be rather heavy for the lax upright growth. It is therefore a good idea to give it support.

Marjorie Fair   Repeat flowering

Parentage   Ballerina × Baby Faurax
Raiser   Harkness
Year of introduction   1978
Carmine-red with a silvery white eye. A red Ballerina-type shrub, and forms a perfect planting companion to that variety. 4–5 ft (1.2–1.5 m).

Nevada   Repeat flowering

Parentage   Given as La Giralda × *R. moyesii* (but this is disputed by many botanists)
Raiser   Dot
Year of introduction   1927
A fine shrub growing to 7–8 ft (2.1–2.5 m) with large open single flowers (often 5 in or more [13 cm or more] across), with prominent golden stamens. Under some weather conditions, the petals can be tinted pink. The smallish, medium green matt foliage may need some protection against Black Spot. 'Marguerite Hilling' is a flushed rose-pink sport of 'Nevada'.

Nozomi   Repeat flowering

Parentage   Fairy Princess × Sweet Fairy
Raiser   Onodera (Japan)
Year of introduction   1972
Small single blooms of pearl pink fading to white, borne in trusses. A spreading, almost flat grower, it can be used as ground cover if pegged down.

Nymphenburg   Repeat flowering

Parentage   Sangerhausen × Sunmist
Raiser   Kordes
Year of introduction   1954
An upright growing 6 ft (1.8 m) shrub Rose. Very double blooms of pale salmon with yellow shade, fragrant.

'Fritz Nobis'.   ▶

Rainbow

Repeat flowering

Parentage Vera Dalton × Buccaneer
Raiser Mattock
Year of introduction 1974
Semi-double blooms of orange with pink and yellow shadings, vigorous spreading habit and dark bronze-green foliage.

Sparrieshoop

Repeat flowering

Parentage (Baby Châteaux × Else Poulsen) × Magnifica
Raiser Kordes
Year of introduction 1953
A tall upright shrub bearing large single blooms of shaded light pink, very fragrant, but some trouble from Black Spot.

Scharlachglut (Scarlet Fire)

Summer flowering

Parentage Poinsettia × Alika
Raiser Kordes
Year of introduction 1952
Large 5 in (13 cm) single flowers of bright scarlet followed by large ornamental heps.

Summer Fields

Repeat flowering

Parentage (Super Star × Evelyn Fison) × seedling
Raiser Mattock
Year of introduction 1971
Semi-double blooms of deep vermilion-rose opening to show bright golden stamens. A bushy shrub Rose growing to 6 ft (1.8 m). Named in honour of the Oxford school in the year of its centennary.

Swany

Repeat flowering

Raiser Meilland
Year of introduction 1978
Small very double snow white blooms in large trusses borne on a low ground hugging plant.

Westerland

Repeat flowering

Raiser Kordes
Year of introduction 1969
Bright golden orange semi-double blooms in large trusses on a vigorous shrub of medium height. The foliage is deep bronze-green.

'Marjorie Fair'. ▶

Species Roses

Of more than one hundred distinct species of Roses collected from the wild, it is thought that possibly only a handful have been used in the breeding of the garden Rose we know. However, several are of sufficient ornamental value in their own right to find a place in the garden. They all have diverse characteristics.

R. ecae

A dainty briar from Afghanistan, discovered by Dr J. Aitchison, a medical officer in the British Army during the second Afghan war and named in honour of his wife, the name being formed by her initials, E.C.A. The small single flowers are of intense yellow and the foliage is of dainty fernlike formation.

R. farreri persetosa

Nicknamed 'The Threepenny Bit Rose' from the tiny single light pink blooms which echoed the size of the old silver coin of that value used in the early part of this century. The bush grows to about 12 ft (3 m) and more and is a veritible thicket of tall upright shoots thickly set with such fine prickles that they resemble bristles. The fernlike foliage is very small but profuse and the dainty blooms are followed by tiny gemlike heps of bright orange-scarlet.

R. filipes var Kiftsgate

Whether this is the true species or a variation, it is an extremely valuable plant for the larger garden as it can grow to enormous proportions. A good subject to grow into trees or hedges where it can scramble to 30 ft (9 m). A mature specimen covered in enormous clusters of very fragrant creamy white single blooms make a spectacular feature, but 'Kiftsgate', named for a famous garden in Gloucestershire, may take four or five years before producing flowers.

R. hugonis

Such a popular wild plant soon gets a popular name, and as well as the obvious 'Father Hugo's Rose', this is known as the 'Golden Rose of China'. Raised from seed gathered towards the end of the nineteenth century by the Rev. Hugh Scallan, a missionary in China and introduced in 1899. The shrub grows to about 15 ft (4 m) in height and is wide-spreading. The creamy yellow cup-shaped flowers are 1 in (4 cm) and are borne in great profusion in late spring amid profuse fernlike foliage.

R. moyesii

An attractive species whose beauty has tempted hybridists and selectors and the forms of this species are much sought after. *R. moyesii fargesii*, *R. moyesii rosea* (also known as *R. holodonta*), *R. × highdownensis*, cultivars, 'Fred Streeter', 'Geranium', and 'Sealing Wax' are among the best known. Discovered by the famed plant collector, Ernest H. Wilson (1876–1930) who named it for the Rev. J. Moyes of the China Inland Mission. The species is tall often 15–18 ft (4–5 m) and the metallic red flowers are extremely regular in their five-petalled arrangements, neatly surrounding the dense ring of bright golden stamens.

R. rugosa rubra ▶

170

R. omeiensis pteracantha

The difference in naming can be quite bewildering – *omeiensis* is the name under which the writer grows it, but the botanists, having changed it from *sericea*, now seem to revert to that name. Whatever the name, the charm of this species makes it a favourite wherever a vast grower is needed. Specimens in the Mattock garden are 18 ft (5 m) high and almost as much through. Grown in China it is said as a cattle fence, one of the oddest features of this briar is that the white flowers have only four petals whereas all other species have five.

R. primula

The 'Incense Rose', a medium growing briar of about 5 ft ($2\frac{1}{2}$ m) in height, The glossy fernlike foliage exudes a delightfully resinous incense-like fragrance when crushed, or into the air as on a warm summer evening. The pale cup-shaped flowers of pale creamy yellow are borne in the early summer.

R. rubrifolia

Cultivated prior to 1820 this briar, native to Central and Eastern Europe, is a favourite foliage plant and is much cultivated in the gardens of flower arrangers. The stems and foliage are a glaucous purple, almost as if they have a bloom like the fruit of the grape. The flowers, insignificant from an ornamental point of view, are important in that in the best forms of the species they are followed by a mass of rich mahogany coloured heps.

R. rugosa (The Ramanas Rose)

From North China, Korea and Japan this is one of the most valued species of the Rose, apart from the ubiquitous Hybrid Tea/Floribunda Rose. Its forms have proved most valuable as an understock, as subjects for amenity planting in landscaping projects, and as a shrub for general garden use. The pink form, *R. rugosa rubra*, and the white-flowered *R. rugosa alba* are most effective in flower and in fruiting. The tomato-shaped heps are borne at the same time as the autumn flowers. The name is taken from the Latin 'ruga', meaning wrinkled, the most obvious adjective to describe the foliage which is normally glossy. The other characteristic of the species being the mass of prickles carried on its shoots.

R. sweginzowii

Rose pink flowers with creamy stamens, are carried the whole length of the vigorous upright stems and are followed by bright scarlet flask-shaped heps. Extremely prickly, the large triangular thorns are scarlet and translucent when young.

R. xanthina

A delightful yellow species, the double form of which is known under the name of *R. slingeri* after the late W. (Billy) Slinger of the famous Donard Nursery in Northern Ireland. The best known form, however, is the cultivar 'Canary Bird'. A delightful shrub, whose fresh green fernlike foliage is set in the spring with single bright yellow flowers. The history of this variety is somewhat obscure, but it would appear to have been discovered on a nursery in Surrey in the early part of this century and to have been seen in many a botanic garden before it became so well known in general commerce.

R. pomifera ▶

Index of Varieties

Figures in **bold** indicate the page numbers of photographs.